50 Ways to Love Your Man

Approaching the Heart with a Rational Mind

Sarah Cline, Ph.D.

Copyright © 2023 Sarah Cline, Ph.D.

All rights reserved.

The contents of this book may not be reproduced, duplicated, or transmitted without direct written permission from the author.

Under no circumstances will any legal responsibility or blame be held against the publisher for any reparation, damages, or monetary loss due to the information herein, either directly or indirectly.

Legal Notice:

This book is copyright-protected. This is only for personal use. You cannot amend, distribute, sell, use, quote, or paraphrase any part of the content within this book without the consent of the author.

Disclaimer Notice:

Please note the information contained within this document is for educational and entertainment purposes only. Every attempt has been made to provide accurate, up-to-date, and reliable complete information. No warranties of any kind are expressed or implied. Readers acknowledge that the author is not engaging in the rendering of legal, financial, medical, or professional advice. The content of this book has been derived from various sources. Please consult a licensed professional before attempting any techniques outlined in this book.

By reading this document, the reader agrees that under no circumstances is the author responsible for any losses, direct or indirect, which are incurred as a result of the use of the information contained within this document, including, but not limited to, errors, omissions, or inaccuracies.

ISBN: 978-1-937209-23-0

Contents

Introduction 1
   The Power of Personalities
   Before We Begin

1. Understanding Your Man's Personality Type 4
   Origins of Personality Types
   Cave Dweller (CD) and Mountain Yeller (MY) Men
   Cave Dweller (CD) Man
   Deeper Dive into the Mountain Yeller (MY) Man
   The Straddler Man
   Key Takeaways

2. Communication Is Key 20
   Express Feelings without Instigating Conflicts
   Appreciate Silence With CDs
   Offer Regular Verbal Affirmations to MYs
   Understand and Respect Personal Boundaries
   Engage in Consistent Relationship Check-Ins
   Embrace Spontaneity
   Regularly Share Personal-Growth Moments
   Key Takeaways

3. Intimacy Insights 36

Recognize Sexual Dynamics
Foster Emotional Connections with CDs
Prioritize Physical Intimacy for MYs
Make Romantic Gestures
Schedule Date Nights
Revisit Relationship Firsts
Write Old-Fashioned Love Letters
Plan Trips and Weekend Getaways
Bond Over Mutual Interests and Hobbies
Discuss Needs and Desires
Key Takeaways

4. Balancing Social Needs   56

Harmonize a CD's Need for Solitude with an MY's Social Inclinations
Plan Activities That Cater to Both Personalities
Gradually Introduce CDs to Intimate Social Settings
Appreciate MY's Need for Broader Social Engagements
Set Boundaries for Personal Space and Time
Engage in Joint Classes or Workshops
Allow Separate Nights Out with Friends
Host Mutual Social Events or Gatherings
Celebrate Milestones Together
Recognize Individual Achievements in Social Groups
Key Takeaways

5. Emotional Harmony   74

Celebrate the Unique Emotional Strengths You Each Offer
Offer Emotional Support to MYs in Their Social Endeavors
Encourage and Understand CDs in Their Introspective Moments

      Navigate Vulnerabilities Together
      Gain Emotional Insights through Books, Movies, and Podcasts
      Key Takeaways

6. Financial Balance   85
      Healthily Navigate Financial Disagreements
      Engage in Joint Financial Planning
      Handle Unsolicited Financial Advice
      Understand Your Partner's Financial Traits and Background
      Celebrate Meaningful Financial and Career Milestones
      Key Takeaways

7. Keep Love Thriving   105
      Renew Your Vows
      Have Occasional "Relationship Holidays"
      Establish Ongoing Relationship Rituals
      Engage in Therapeutic Activities Together
      Participate in Couples' Counseling and Enrichment
      Discover New Activities and Pursuits Together
      Support and Share in Individual Dreams and Aspirations
      Respect and Encourage Personal Growth
      Revisit Meaningful Places from Your Shared History
      Celebrate Anniversaries and Special Occasions
      Key Takeaways

8. Final Thoughts   128
      Understanding the Depth of Personality
      The Journey of Mutual Growth
      The Evolution of Your Love Story

Appendices   131

Introduction

Welcome to *50 Ways to Love Your Man.* If you've picked up this book, you may be in a challenging relationship, eager to enhance an existing bond, or just gearing up for what the future holds in your romantic life. Whatever the case, you've taken a significant step toward deeper understanding and connection—so, congratulations are in order.

Throughout this volume and larger series, we'll focus on three universal personality categories: the reserved Cave Dweller (CD), the outgoing Mountain Yeller (MY), and the Straddler, who exhibits mixed traits. Recognizing and understanding these types is crucial, as they shape relationship dynamics in untold ways. Our aim is to provide practical insights into fundamental personalities, ensuring you're better equipped to navigate and strengthen your relationships. What's more, you'll walk away with a better grasp of who you truly are—and by knowing ourselves, we're better for others.

Armed with the insights from this book, you'll not only interpret actions but also understand the deeper motivations behind them with greater ease. Prepare to see your man—and perhaps yourself—in a whole new light...

The Power of Personalities

Ahead, we'll demystify the core attributes of CDs, MYs, and Straddlers, equipping you with insights to comprehend and appreciate the nuances of each type. Appreciating these differences allows you to interpret your man's behaviors accurately within his unique personality context, thus avoiding flawed assumptions.

Too often in relationships, we mistakenly attribute conflicts and misunderstandings to a lack of love, empathy, or respect. Yet, more frequently, it's a simple gap in understanding. When we don't perceive the underlying personality traits driving our partners' actions, we can misinterpret their intentions, leading to undue tension. It's not always about agreeing or having the same viewpoint; it's about acknowledging and respecting these inherent differences. By recognizing the core personality traits of CDs, MYs, and Straddlers, we can better empathize with our partners, allowing love to fully flourish.

Before We Begin

50 Ways to Love Your Man offers no quick fix or casual checklist. Instead, it emphasizes "love" as an active endeavor, demanding both attention and effort. While you'll find a great deal of guidance here, it's up to you to apply these insights authentically.

Engaging with this material will require introspection, and there will be moments that challenge your current understanding of relationships—and everything else. Yet, it's in these times of reflection and adjustment that true growth happens... and, here, the fruits of your labor could scarcely be sweeter—some real incentive.

Through patience and ongoing application, you're not just enhancing a single bond but, rather, refining how you connect. How you live. How you share your soul. So, love the process, love yourself, and love your man on a whole new level.

Before we begin, remind yourself: you're a masterpiece—and a work in progress.

Chapter One

Understanding Your Man's Personality Type

Do you find yourself struggling to understand your male partner's personality traits? Are you frustrated that they're so dissimilar to yours? Chances are, when you first met your man, you enjoyed the differences he brought to the table. But once the honeymoon period was over, it's likely that those differences became a source of frustration, misunderstanding, and even strife.

Understanding personality types is an essential piece of the puzzle when seeking to understand your man. Appreciating your partner means discovering their many layers and complexities, and all of them should garner your attention if you are to experience a happy and healthy relationship.

In this chapter, we will discuss the personality types of the Cave Dweller man, which we will refer to as CD man, the Mountain Yeller or MY man, and the Straddler man. Learning about these three basic personality types will give you a clearer picture of the unique benefits and challenges each creates. And understanding is an essential first step to bringing harmony and happiness into your everyday life.

Origins of Personality Types

Long before the modern-day classifications of CDs and MYs and even before psychiatrists and psychologists stepped onto the scene, ancient civilizations sought to explain human behavior and its various nuances.

The Ancient Greeks

The ancient Greeks developed the theory of "four humors" to explain the causes of health and illness, both mental and physical. This theory suggested that an individual's temperament was influenced by bodily fluids: blood (sanguine), yellow bile (choleric), black bile (melancholic), and phlegm (phlegmatic). The Greeks thought these humors were directly related to being sanguine (cheerful), choleric (short-tempered), melancholic (reserved), or phlegmatic (relaxed). Therefore, the balance of these humors was believed to influence an individual's temperament, health, and overall disposition. While an imbalance of these humors led to behaviors that, today, we associate with certain mental illnesses. For example:

- Sanguine (blood) was associated with cheerful, optimistic, enthusiastic personality traits. An imbalance was thought to be due to a person having too much blood in their body, which would cause a person to be overly confident and have impulsive behavior. Possible narcissistic and/or bipolar disorder.

- Choleric (yellow bile) was associated with being ambitious, passionate, and easily angered. An imbalance causes anger, irritability, or extremely aggressive behavior and rage. Possible borderline personality disorder.

- Melancholic (black bile) was associated with being thoughtful, reflective, and often sad or depressed. This imbalance was associated with melancholy and depression.

- Phlegmatic (phlegm) was associated with being calm, reliable, and often unemotional or apathetic. An imbalance was associated with lethargy, sluggishness, or a lack of motivation, which, much like melancholic, is a symptom of depression.

Treating these emotional ailments is where things got even more interesting. If the Greeks thought you had an imbalance of any of these four humors, you would likely have received one of the following treatments:

Dietary Changes: Prescribed depending on the humor in excess. For instance, someone deemed overly choleric might be advised to avoid hot or spicy foods that would "agitate" the yellow bile.

Bloodletting: If you were someone believed to have an excess of sanguine humor, it was common practice to be prescribed bloodletting. This process involved removing blood from the body by way of leeches or actual cutting.

Purging: In order to remove excess bile or phlegm, laxatives were used, as were emetics, which induced vomiting.

Baths/Sweating: To promote toxin removal, balms and ointments were applied to the skin to help with the imbalance of any of these four humors.

The Greeks' attempts to "treat" imbalances in personality or health were based on the observations and the knowledge they had at the time. The four humors theory was eventually replaced with more accurate medical models, but its influence can still be seen in some of our languages today.

The Introvert and The Extrovert

Carl Gustav Jung (1875–1961) was a Swiss psychiatrist, psychoanalyst, and the father of analytical psychology. He developed several concepts that had a profound influence on both psychology and popular culture. One of his most notable contributions was the concept of "introversion" and "extraversion" (often used in the more modern manner: introvert and extrovert). Jung's theory asserts that introversion and extraversion are attitudes that represent the direction in which a person's psychic energy flows.

Extraversion (Extrovert)

According to Jung, the extrovert's energy flows outward. This personality type is more oriented toward the external world and derives energy from interacting with its surroundings, including people, events, and situations. If your man is an extrovert, he tends to be more outgoing, social, and interested in external events. He is typically action-oriented and is generally more comfortable in social situations than an introverted man. Many extroverts are highly influenced by external factors and are occasionally prone to negative introspection.

Introversion (Introvert)

As the name suggests, the introvert's energy flows inward. This personality type is more oriented toward his inner world, relying on introspection and internal reflection. If your partner is introverted, he is generally more reserved and often feels more comfortable with individual activities or smaller group settings. He derives energy and pleasure from thinking, daydreaming, or exploring ideas. Although an introverted man's daily practices tend to lead to social isolation, many have a small number of deep connections with people of their choosing.

Jung believed that everyone has an introverted and extroverted side, with one being more dominant than the other. It's a spectrum, and while some men might be near the extremes of that spectrum, most individuals lie somewhere in between.

Cave Dweller (CD) and Mountain Yeller (MY) Men

While not strictly rooted in these historical contexts, the CD and MY classifications are evolved constructs reflecting the same human desire to understand ourselves and others in our world more deeply.

While our contemporary understanding of the CD and MY classifications doesn't stem directly from ancient Greek or Jungian theories, much like their historical counterparts, they are observed patterns in modern relationships. By identifying recurring patterns, we can forge tools to help us navigate and harmonize interpersonal interactions.

Cave Dweller (CD) Man

To determine whether you and your man fall into the CD or MY category, we must first learn about their traits.

Reserved Nature

If your man is a CD, he will predominantly showcase a calm and reserved demeanor. He is introspective and tends to hold his emotions close to his chest because he values his inner world and the sanctuary it provides. His reserved nature doesn't mean that he is indifferent or doesn't care about his partner; it just means that he processes his emotions internally and over time.

For instance, after an argument, a CD man might choose to withdraw to process his feelings rather than immediately confront an issue. A CD man does this because he typically feels uncomfortable with strife and needs time to work through his emotions and how to communicate his feelings.

Socially, a CD man is often found in quieter corners, engaging in deep conversation with one or two individuals rather than in the center of a party. In group discussions, a CD will offer insights only if specifically asked or if he feels strongly about a topic.

Logical Thinking and Literal Communication

A CD man leans more toward analytical and logical thinking. He makes decisions only after careful contemplation and weighing the pros and cons. He works hard to keep his emotions from clouding his judgment. This logical thinking manifests in his communication, as he will get right to the point without inserting emotions or using stories to embellish his point.

For example, if you discuss a film with a CD man, he will likely dissect plot points with impeccable logic and even point out strengths and weaknesses. But he often misses the emotional undertones of the movie. If you ask a CD if he liked the cake you brought for dessert, he might reply, "Yes," without diving into flowery descriptives.

It's important to note that a CD man may also get frustrated with an embellished story that doesn't immediately get to the point. It doesn't mean he doesn't want to hear the story or doesn't care what the person has to say; his brain is just geared toward immediate outcomes.

Need for Space

A CD man has an inherent need for both emotional and physical personal space. For him, requiring space is not about distancing himself from loved ones. It's about needing solitude to recharge and reflect.

CD men enjoy reading books in a cozy nook or going for solitary walks. They may listen to music while cooking dinner instead of talking. This alone time is essential for a CD man, especially after a day filled with social interactions.

Singular Focus

A CD man has unparalleled concentration when engrossed in a task and prefers completing that task to his satisfaction before tackling another.

If you attempt to talk to a CD man while he's writing an email, for example, he may be so absorbed in what he's writing that you'll be tuned out. It's not that what you're saying is unimportant to him; it's just challenging for him to spread his focus on more than one thing at a time because he gives each item his full attention.

Social Preferences

Traditionally, if your man were labeled an introvert, many would also consider him anti-social. But that couldn't be further from the truth. An introvert, or a CD man, just leans toward more intimate social interactions. Large gatherings can leave a CD man feeling overwhelmed and quickly drain his mental and emotional battery.

Emotional Processing

While CD men might not outwardly express their emotions, they experience them deeply. However, their internal reflections may lead to a delay in their outward emotional expression. While a CD man may seem distant after an emotional confrontation, many need to process the interaction before they react. A CD man needs time to contemplate a disagreement, analyze the conversation, and figure out where things went wrong before he can move on to a resolution. This meditation is essential for a CD man's counterpart to understand; the more they push a CD man to express himself, the more he will clam up in response.

Fears Regarding Loss of Security

Finally, if your man is a CD, he craves stability in his life, especially his finances. He will likely be frugal in his spending and make decisions with the lowest level of risk. At times, a CD man may pick a job over family, not because he loves to work more, but because he needs security above all else. The hierarchy of basic needs for a CD man is as follows:

- Career/Financial Security
- Hobbies/Children
- Relationships/Family
- Sex/Lovers

The position of each need doesn't mean they don't love and value their partner/family. It means that it's essential for a CD man to feel that he's providing security for himself and his family before he can give his full attention to the next set of needs.

Deeper Dive into the Mountain Yeller (MY) Man

If your man is an extrovert, chances are he's been called that more than once in his lifetime. An extrovert is typically known for being outgoing and the life of any party. But there's so much more to them than meets the eye.

Outgoing Nature/Group Socialization

An MY man is inherently outgoing. His energy thrives on interactions and being around people as often as possible. Instead of needing time alone to recharge, an MY man wants to be out and involved.

At a social event, MY men will be the first to initiate games and dancing and will often bounce from person to person, catching up rather than focusing on one task at a time. Deep conversations are still on the table but not at a social event. MY men are usually the ones who rally their friends for a group outing over a weekend rather than sitting at home reading a book or watching TV. Even in the workplace, MY men love group projects and find collaborative brainstorming and teamwork exciting.

Emotion-Driven

MY men are heart-ruled because they lead with their intuition and emotions. Being ruled by their heart doesn't mean their decisions are devoid of logic, but their feelings heavily influence their reactions. MY men can be emotional during arguments but are also the first to send a heartfelt message to a friend upon hearing they are having a rough time.

An MY man's emotions will show throughout his storytelling, so be patient when he tells you about an event or relays the plot to a movie. Chances are both will be full of details and embellishments.

Connection and Touch

MY men crave genuine connections and physical touch. Whether a hug, a pat on the back, or simply holding hands. It reinforces their feeling of being connected. In a relationship, the MY man will crave physical affection and see it as a top priority over other needs—something we'll discuss in depth a bit later.

Dynamic Focus

The MY man is a natural multitasker. Instead of focusing on one task at a time, his attention shifts between assignments. He enjoys the energy he gets from juggling multiple things and often gets bored working on one project for an extended period. It can be common to find the MY man drifting off during a long presentation. He's busy thinking about weekend plans.

The MY man doesn't mind dealing with paperwork, but he'll work through it while watching television or listening to music. As for conversations, the MY man loves to chat, but don't be surprised if you find the MY man scrolling on his phone while talking with you. It's not that the MY man thinks what you have to say is unimportant. His mind simply runs at higher speeds, and he's more comfortable when processing more than one thing at a time.

Inferential Communication

The MY man often communicates using stories, anecdotes, and metaphors rather than getting straight to the point. He relies on indirect implications and expects others to infer meanings, which can confuse some who may not be familiar with his communication style.

During an argument, the partner of an MY man may find it hard to decipher what the MY man really wants, even if he feels he has told them directly. It's essential to have a middle ground where communication is concerned, especially if your man is an MY trying to get through to a CD. Their communication styles are very different.

Immediate Emotional Expression

Unlike their CD counterparts, MY men are quick to express their emotions. They're an open book and rarely hesitate to share their feelings of joy and disappointment. This can be overwhelming for a CD who is uncomfortable with an emotional display.

One of the greatest fears the MY man faces is the fear of rejection. If an MY man has a CD partner, who usually pulls away at any sign of conflict, this can be a bone of contention. The MY man will take your withdrawal as a sign of personal rejection. It's important to communicate that you are not rejecting him and that you simply need time to wrap your head around and process the disagreement. Give the MY man verbal and physical affirmations whenever possible.

The hierarchy of basic needs for the MY man is as follows:

- Relationships/Sex
- Family/Children
- Friends/Hobbies
- Career/Financial Security

If you are a CD and your partner is an MY, don't panic; it doesn't mean you cannot have a successful relationship. There are plenty of amazing and fulfilling relationships between opposites. It just means it will take time, work, and patience to learn one another's needs and effectively communicate.

The Straddler Man

If your man is a Straddler, he is adaptable and enjoys the best of both worlds. He can immerse himself in a book like a CD man or be the life of a party like the MY man. He possesses an emotional agility that allows him to straddle his personality types seamlessly. While this book predominantly focuses on CD and MY men, Straddlers can use it to understand the extremes and navigate their middle ground more effectively.

Excellent Balance Between Reflection and Expression

A Straddler man can introspect like a CD, valuing quiet moments of thought. Yet, he also appreciates the expressive vitality of the MY and shares his feelings and ideas openly when a situation calls for it. He is as happy spending a quiet evening reading as he is going to a book club and actively participating in a lively discussion.

Adaptable in Social Situations

While he might not always be the life of the party, he easily adjusts to situations based on the social settings and the company involved. He can engage in a one-on-one conversation at a party and then join a group game or be the center of the party later in the evening.

Values Both Logic and Emotion

A Straddler man approaches situations with a logical mindset but is equally attuned to the emotional undercurrents, valuing the importance of feelings in decision-making. For example, if a colleague faces a personal issue, the Straddler man will offer practical solutions while simultaneously providing emotional support.

Flexibility in Needs and Fears

The Straddler man's hierarchy of needs will fluctuate based on circumstances, and he might experience fears from the CD's spectrum, such as loss of security, as well as the MY's fear of rejection. However, adaptability allows him to prioritize different aspects of his life. While working on an important business project, he will prioritize career stability, but in his downtime, he will focus on relationships and personal connections.

Fluid Communication Styles

A Straddler man can communicate both directly and inferentially, often adjusting his communication based on the recipient. For example, when conversing with his analytical boss, he will be direct and to the point, but when he talks to his best friend, he becomes expressive and delves into all the nitty-gritty details.

Straddlers possess an innate ability to mediate and find common ground, especially in relationships where CDs and MYs might find themselves at odds. His adaptability enables him to comprehend and empathize with both personality types, easing communication and diminishing misunderstandings.

A Straddler man and his partner may seem like a perfect match. However, everyone encounters their share of struggles. The flexibility of a Straddler often causes confusion about his preferences and needs. He might sometimes feel stretched or trapped in the middle, particularly in a polarized situation where he wishes to please his partner and struggles to voice his disagreements. A Straddler man must discern what is truly significant to him while also learning to navigate his partner's personality type, much like everyone else.

So, How Do You Find Common Ground?

I'm a CD, and my partner is an MY. Is my relationship doomed?

Absolutely not! In this book, we don't tell you how to "cope" with your partner's differences. We provide you with the ability to realize the unique strengths each person brings to a relationship. A CD's introspection can balance an MY's spontaneity. An MY's vivacity and exuberance can harmonize beautifully with a CD's depth and stability.

Recognizing these different traits is merely the first step to a healthy relationship. The real challenge, and indeed the focus of this book, is to find ways to navigate the complexities of these interactions. After all, the beauty of a relationship truly unfolds in the dance between these personalities.

Key Takeaways

Diving into the intricacies of personality types isn't about affixing labels but rather enriching our understanding. With these insights, you're now armed with the necessary vocabulary to navigate the labyrinth of human emotions and connections, fostering an environment where love thrives, understanding blossoms, and relationships flourish. As we embark on this journey, let's remember that the goal isn't to change but to adapt, understand, and love more deeply.

The foundation for a nurturing relationship starts with understanding—understanding yourself, your partner, and the dynamics of your interaction. With the knowledge of CD and MY personality traits, you're well on your way to deepening that understanding, setting the stage for the subsequent chapters that will guide you on how to cherish your partner in ways that resonate with both of you.

Understanding personality differences is essential for nurturing compatibility. This chapter has illuminated the fundamental traits of CDs, MYs, and Straddlers.

- **Reserved Nature:** Respect your CD partner's need for personal space and quiet reflection. Don't force immediate emotional reactions.

- **Logical Thinking:** Recognize your CD partner's analytical approach. Be patient as they process before expressing feelings.

- **Singular Focus:** Acknowledge that multitasking is difficult for your CD partner. Allow them to complete or pause their task before they give you their full attention.

- **Emotion-Driven:** Empathize with your MY partner's emotions. Give your man positive affirmations/compliments and physical affection.

- **Inferential Communication:** Listen for meanings implied indirectly in your MY partner's stories. Learn to read between the lines.

- **Dynamic Focus:** Accept your MY partner's wandering attention. Multitasking is their nature. If you need their full focus, tell them.

- **Excellent Balance:** Appreciate the adaptability of a Straddler partner. Avoid putting them in the middle of conflicts.

- **Flexible Needs:** Accommodate shifts in a Straddler partner's priorities. Reassure them of your unconditional love.

The key is learning your dance as a couple. When personalities harmonize through understanding and respect, relationships flourish.

Chapter Two

Communication Is Key

Effective communication is the foundation of any healthy relationship, regardless of personality type. It's the bridge that connects CDs and MYs, enabling mutual understanding. In this chapter, we'll delve into the essential components of communication that can strengthen your bond. Moreover, we'll navigate the unique traits of each personality type and how you can use personality indicators to validate your man and his needs.

While it's easy to be swayed by the idea that love is a mysterious force beyond our control, the reality is that maintaining a lasting relationship requires conscious effort, respect, and a willingness to understand. This journey of appreciation goes beyond knowing your man's favorite "things." It's about diving deep into their psyche, comprehending their personality traits, and recognizing how these soul-deep attributes interact with your own.

In the age of digital connections and instant gratification, we sometimes forget the beauty of genuine human interaction. We often overlook the importance of patience, reflection, and being present with our loved ones. Thus, as we progress through this chapter, you're invited to pause, reflect, and feel. By fostering an environment of open communication and mutual respect, you're not just building a relationship but cultivating a partnership that thrives on understanding, compassion, and genuine connection. Here are some strategies and ground rules to help you convey your emotions effectively:

Express Feelings without Instigating Conflicts

Expressing your feelings is crucial for any relationship, but it's essential to do so without triggering conflicts. It's all too easy to get wrapped up in emotions when expressing them to someone else—especially when you're first sorting through them—so, it's crucial to first take a step back, breathe, and formulate thoughts before verbalizing them.

Remain Calm

Try not to overreact to difficult situations. By remaining calm, it's more likely that your man will feel like he has the space and ability to consider your perspective.

Express Feelings with Words, Not Actions

If you start to get angry and feel you may lose control, take a break and do something to help yourself feel calm.

- Take a walk

- Do breathing exercises

- Interact with a pet

- Journal
- Read a book

Address One Issue at a Time

Don't introduce tertiary issues until the primary problem has been fully discussed. This way, you'll avoid what experts call the "kitchen sink effect." This term was coined by Dr. John Mordechai Gottman (born April 26, 1942), an American psychologist and professor at the University of Washington, whose work focused on divorce prediction and marital stability. The phrase describes the act of one partner throwing "everything but the kitchen sink" into an argument by dredging up past mistakes and grievances. This tactic is particularly counterproductive, as it's often overwhelming to the partner receiving the grievances.

Mitigate the Kitchen Sink Effect

When emotions flare up, it's natural to fall back on old hurt feelings—especially if they're similar to current difficulties.

- One of the most common reasons for someone to resort to "kitchen sinking" is quite simple: to win the argument. However, this amounts to "winning the battle but losing the war." It's a surefire way to sabotage potential progress in your relationship.

- Poor communication skills can also be to blame. Sometimes, a person doesn't realize they're being destructive by doing this, never having learned how to express and work through past feelings of hurt in a healthy manner.

Fixating on past mistakes is almost always counterproductive. Your man may feel bullied, overwhelmed, or even blindsided by the onslaught of criticisms, especially if the argument is over something else entirely. If you resort to this tactic, it's indicative of avoidance. So, ask yourself: are you dodging the real issue at hand?

Instead of resorting to this method, remain calm and employ effective communication techniques. You don't want to bully your man, no matter how angry you may be. Easier said than done, of course! It's a difficult habit to break, but if you find yourself participating in this behavior, the most important thing to do is remain aware and calm. If you value your relationship and want to move forward, choose your words mindfully and let go of past transgressions.

Resist Underhandedness

Avoid hitting below the belt or being underhanded. Never use these conversations to attack your partner—especially in sensitive areas. These attacks only foster distrust, anger, and harmful vulnerability. We don't want to "win" arguments. We want to work through issues by effectively communicating. Remember, it's not you vs. your partner. It is you and your partner vs. the problem.

Avoid Clamming Up

Positive results can only be obtained by way of proper communication. It's easy to feel emotionally charged when discussing your feelings with your partner, especially if they've upset you or you think they're upset with you. Often, when emotions run high, we "clam up" or shut down.

It's important to note that when one person becomes silent and stops responding to the other, frustration and anger can be the result. If you feel yourself getting overwhelmed or shutting down, you may need to take a break from the discussion. Just let him know you'll return to the conversation as soon as you're able to do so, and then don't forget to follow up. Follow-up is essential. Keep your promise and return to the conversation. You may even want to refer back to the "remain calm" section to recenter for the next discussion.

Likewise, if you notice your man is clamming up, offer to circle back later to give them time to reset.

Be Specific and Productive

Be precise about what's bothering you. Try not to generalize. Avoid words like "never" or "always." These sweeping terms are usually inaccurate anyway and will (almost) always heighten tensions. Instead of using hyperbolic language that could cause your man to feel powerless, focus on what you're feeling in the moment. Vague complaints are also challenging to address, and it's important to tackle each specific item productively.

Prioritize Active Listening

Practice active listening when your partner tells you something important, and avoid interrupting them when they're speaking, even if you disagree. Active listening is the cornerstone of all effective communication. It involves not only hearing the words your partner says but also understanding his emotions and perspectives. Validate your partner by maintaining eye contact and providing non-verbal cues like nodding to show that you're engaged. Our body language matters.

Be present in the conversation, and take your man's feelings and criticisms seriously. Don't be distracted by external forces. Never multi-task while your man is communicating. Put down those dishes. Put away your phone. If it takes your eyes or thoughts away from him, don't engage in the activity. Listen to and reflect on what he is saying before responding. Be sure to ask open-ended questions to encourage him to share more, and remember one thing: if he's communicating it, it's important.

Use Neutral Language to Curb Defensiveness

Your choice of words can significantly impact the tone of your communication. To prevent defensiveness and promote understanding, avoid accusatory language and instead focus on the specific behavior or issue. Accusations will lead your man to focus on defending himself rather than on understanding you and your perspective. Instead, discuss how an action made you feel.

Use "We" Statements

Using "we" instead of "you" statements conveys that you are in this together, working as a team to resolve the problem. It's important to communicate that you are practicing empathy and acknowledging each other's feelings and perspectives to maintain a harmonious relationship.

For instance, if the issue is about one partner feeling overwhelmed with household responsibilities, using "we" statements can help you address the concern without making the other partner feel accused.

Don't Say This:
"You never help me with the household chores."

Instead, Say This:
"We seem to have a lot of chores piling up, and it's becoming overwhelming. Can we find a way to share the responsibilities more equally so we both have time to relax?"

Emphasizing "we" makes the conversation more about finding solutions together rather than pointing fingers, which can often lead to a more productive and less confrontational discussion.

Use "I" Statements

When faced with a conflict, expressing yourself without becoming overly aggressive can be challenging. To help de-escalate the situation and clarify your point, an "I" statement—or an assertive statement—is an effective psychiatrist-approved approach. Suppose there's a conflict where one partner feels neglected because the other partner spends a lot of time working and not paying enough attention to them.

Don't Say This:
"You are always working and never spend any time with me! You don't care about our relationship."

Instead, Say This:
"I feel neglected when you spend a lot of time working, and we don't get to spend quality time together. I value our relationship and would like us to find a balance that allows us to enjoy each other's company."

This "I" statement expresses the speaker's feelings and needs without blaming or accusing the other person, thus making it more likely to result in a productive conversation rather than an argument.

Using language that emphasizes how you feel is much more effective communication and is less likely to result in your man shutting down or getting angry. It also aids in your partner's ability to empathize and see things from your perspective. Here's another example:

Don't Say This:
"You never do the dishes." (This is also likely a generalization.)

Instead, Say This:
"I feel frustrated when I come home and find the sink full of dishes—because I want to come home to a clean space. I would like it if we work on this together."

Speaking this way avoids tactics of attack, critique, and criticism, which usually lead to more hostility and defensiveness. In general, using "I" messages can create a constructive dialogue about the true causes of any conflict by avoiding aggressive behaviors and fostering effective communication.

Appreciate Silence With CDs

For the CD man, silence is often a way to process their thoughts and emotions. It's essential to appreciate and understand this aspect of their communication style:

- Allow your CD partner the time they need to gather their thoughts before discussing important matters.

- Avoid pressuring him to speak immediately after a conflict; they may need time to reflect.

- Create a safe space where silence is not perceived as a negative response but as a part of the communication process.

Offer Regular Verbal Affirmations to MYs

MY men thrive on verbal affirmations and emotional expression. Here's how to make your MY boyfriend or husband feel valued and loved:

- Compliment them genuinely and frequently, acknowledging their strengths and positive qualities.

- Express your love verbally with affectionate language.

- Communicate your appreciation for their efforts and ongoing support

Understand and Respect Personal Boundaries

Both CDs and MYs have distinct personal boundaries. Respecting these boundaries is vital to a harmonious relationship. Therefore, it's important to have open and honest discussions about your respective boundaries and comfort zones. You shouldn't push your partner beyond their comfort zone, whether they need personal space or social engagement—even if this level of care conflicts with your own needs. Creating a balance that respects both partners and their needs for personal growth and reflection is a critical step in communicating and growing with each other. Establishing ground rules regarding when to compromise is a great idea when setting personal boundaries with one another.

Engage in Consistent Relationship Check-Ins

Regular relationship check-ins provide a platform to address concerns and strengthen your connection. These can be every night, once a week, or once a month. Whatever you both choose it's important to schedule a dedicated time for these check-ins to ensure they happen consistently (or happen at all). It's also imperative that these check-ins touch on the positive aspects of your relationship in addition to concerns. Specialists strongly recommend that each of you share something positive about the other when having these discussions. After you've shared the positives and the things you appreciate about one another, leave time for an open and honest talk, allowing you to address the areas that need improvement. Be open to feedback, actively work together, and make necessary adjustments.

How Do You Do a Relationship Check-In?

Pick a Regular Time

Ideally, you'll both be relaxed, present, and in a good mood, so don't schedule a check-in after a long day at work or when you're short on time. You want to bring your best attitude and a clear mindset to these meetings with your partner.

Set the Scene

Your relationship check-in is an opportunity to slow down and connect, so why not make it feel a little special? To that end, bring your favorite snacks and drinks—and conduct the check-in somewhere that feels good to both of you. It needs to be a private and secluded atmosphere, so you both feel comfortable getting real. Ordering take-out and planning something relaxing to do afterward can also help set the mood. And keep in mind that it is encouraged to have these conversations without the influence of alcohol.

Set a Time Limit

You don't want this to become a huge time sink, and you never want it to feel like a chore, so aim for a manageable timescale, especially in the beginning. These check-ins are about opening the lines of communication in a safe and calm manner; you might not resolve everything all at once. Rather, it allows you to create healthy boundaries when expressing vulnerabilities in every facet of your relationship.

Celebrate and Appreciate Each Other

Always start with the positives of your relationship. This appreciation helps each partner remember why they're doing all of this in the first place! Giving compliments and joyful feedback upfront helps your partner feel comfortable and valued. This is especially necessary if there are more challenging topics to discuss afterward. Appreciation and validation are essential ingredients for a quality relationship.

Always Finish on a High Point

A celebration, even a small one, can be a fun way to wrap up the check-in. Remember, these check-ins aren't meant to regurgitate everything your partner has done wrong since your last check-in. As such, it's advisable to maintain regular conversations as tensions or disagreements arise. Otherwise, your check-in may be a powder keg next to an open flame—not good! Also, remember to end the session with a physical touch or an affirmation. Even if things get a little tense or something feels unresolved, find a way to come back to each other and your overall belief in the relationship. If you're checking in regularly and discussing action items as they crop up, it's clear that your relationship is worth believing in.

Schedule Personal Time for Reflection and Understanding

Allocating time for personal reflection and understanding enhances self-awareness and empathy. It gives proper time for each person in the partnership to discover their unique needs, as well as their strengths and weaknesses. Admitting personal faults to ourselves—let alone others—isn't easy. So, consider setting aside moments for self-reflection. Specialists also recommend you journal these thoughts to better understand your emotions and to have the ability to look back at your progress. Encourage your partner to do the same, and share your insights with each other when you're ready.

Use this personal time to explore your progress and how those advancements align with your partner's journey of self-awareness. Self-awareness refers to a clear understanding of your own emotions, strengths, weaknesses, thoughts, and beliefs—and how they might influence your behavior, including your interactions with your partner. Being self-aware is fundamental for healthy relationships with yourself and others—especially your romantic ones. Understanding ourselves means understanding our needs, expectations, boundaries, and communication styles. All of these shape how we interact and love our partners. When we're not self-aware, we open the door to harmful interactions due to blind spots in our communication and waning emotional health. A lack of self-awareness can lead to:

- Poor emotional regulation resulting in outbursts and other unhealthy expressions of anger or hurt.

- Personal neglect and impaired mental health.

- A skewed perception of reality due to biases and defense mechanisms that build up over time. (Also, without self-awareness, a person tends to reject constructive criticism, thus missing out on potential personal growth.)

- Communication blind spots.

- Crossing boundaries—whether your own boundaries or your man's.

Being more self-aware gives us the tools necessary to have satisfying and successful relationships. It just makes sense. Know yourself, and you'll have the foundation for a life and relationship that isn't just surviving but thriving.

Embrace Spontaneity

Spontaneous gestures and surprises can add excitement to your relationship, particularly for MY men who appreciate such acts. Ways to embrace spontaneity include surprise outings or planning activities without revealing all the details in advance. Even if you know what will happen this time, perhaps your man will reciprocate next time. Express your affection unexpectedly through notes, small gifts, and random acts of kindness. Your partner will appreciate the effort involved, and if they're especially fond of surprises, this could help them feel seen and validated.

Regularly Share Personal-Growth Moments

Using feedback obtained from your scheduled meetings, emotional discussions, and self-awareness exercises, you can begin to document your personal development. Once again, journaling is a great way to record feedback and your own reflections. It can provide a glimpse of previous versions of yourself and give greater insight into your personal growth.

Personal growth is an ongoing journey, and sharing these moments of realization—even epiphanies—with your partner can deepen your connection with your man. Discuss your personal experiences, challenges, and lessons learned through self-reflection and check-ins with your partner. Nothing feels better than knowing we've helped someone, so when your man helps, be sure to tell him!

Along the way, support each other's aspirations and encourage continued self-improvement exercises. Then, go on to celebrate milestones in your personal development journey together. By following these guidelines and strategies, you can improve your communication with your partner, whether they're a CD or an MY. Effective communication is the key to understanding, empathy, and building a strong and thriving relationship.

Key Takeaways

Effective communication forms the cornerstone of all healthy and flourishing relationships. It goes beyond the confines of personality types. This chapter has explored the fundamental facets of communication you can use to engage with your partner on a deeper level, whether they exhibit characteristics of CD or MY.

Beyond specific personalities, whether CD or MY, communication is the vital link that connects two souls—so never underestimate its importance.

- **Express, Don't Explode:** Voicing feelings is vital, but how you do it can make or break a conversation. Steer clear of the "kitchen sink" approach and tackle one concern at a time.

- **Listen and Hear:** True listening goes beyond catching words. It's about diving deep, reading between the lines, and feeling the heartbeat behind superficial language.

- **Narrate Neutrally:** Use "I" and "we" statements. These aren't just words; they're bridges that ensure your message gets across without raising defenses.

- **Pivot Your Personality:** Recognize the silence savored by CDs as their reflection time, and shower MYs with affirmations that resonate.

- **Establish Clear Boundaries:** Establish them. Acknowledge them. Respect them. If they're different from yours, that's all right. Find the middle ground through open conversation.

- **Write Relationship Report Cards:** Periodic check-ins keep the ship steady. Use them as reflection mirrors, not boxing rings. And when solitude calls, answer—it fosters self-awareness.

- **Dance Freely:** Sometimes, unplanned moments make the most treasured memories. A little surprise can sprinkle in a whole lot of magic.

- **Share, Grow, Connect:** Sharing personal growth stories isn't just about telling tales—it's about weaving your growth narratives together.

Remember, it's not about speaking the loudest but resonating the deepest. Effective communication is the only way to proper understanding, empathy, and establishing a robust, healthy partnership. By applying these strategies, you can—and will—cultivate a more profound connection with your man. As they say, it takes two to tango, and being conscious of your partner's steps is paramount!

Chapter Three
Intimacy Insights

Romantic relationships truly flourish when both partners engage in persistent efforts to cultivate and enhance intimacy. The initial spark and attraction are integral, forming the base of the relationship; however, the journey to achieve enduring intimacy is an active, continual investment in each other—well beyond the initial phases of blissful infatuation. By understanding and acknowledging your man's, unique personality type, you gain insightful keys to unlocking deeper and more meaningful intimacy that can withstand the test of time.

In this chapter, we'll explore a variety of insightful strategies tailored to CDs and MYs, with the sole objective of intensifying the emotional and physical bonds between partners. By embracing innovative and thoughtful ways to surprise and cherish each other—and by forging stronger bonds—you provide your partner with tangible affirmations of love, thereby ensuring the flame of romance and connection continues to burn brightly.

Recognize Sexual Dynamics

CDs and MYs often have divergent needs and tendencies when it comes to physical intimacy. Recognizing and bridging these gaps is key to promoting mutual satisfaction. It's not just about touch; it's about understanding and alignment.

In any relationship, physical intimacy isn't just a bonus; it's core. It signifies trust, mutual respect, and a shared rhythm. However, diving headfirst into it can be misleading. Instead, it's worth taking a step back and thinking about how we approach it.

One crucial aspect to consider is the unique perspectives of MYs and CDs when it comes to sex. For MYs, sex with their significant others is seen as an expression of love, a vital connection that strengthens their emotional bond. However, it's different for CDs, whose sexual needs tend to be less frequent, often averaging about three days a month, following a more predictable rhythm.

In the case of a relationship where a MY partner is involved with a CD, understanding these differences is essential. MYs may interpret infrequent intimacy as rejection or even suspect their CD partners of infidelity. As such, open and honest communication is paramount. CD partners can reassure MYs of their commitment and emphasize their unique way of expressing love and connection.

By recognizing these distinctions and discussing them openly, both partners can find a middle ground that respects each other's needs and strengthens the foundation of their relationship. Genuine intimacy isn't just about the act; it's about the pact—a shared commitment to understanding and accommodating each other's perspectives and desires.

Connect Intimacy and Emotion for CDs

For the logical CD man, sex may be just one facet of a broader relationship, not the core focus. He sees intimacy as the icing, not the cake itself. His partner's constant advances in lovemaking may feel distracting or premature when he is absorbed in something else. Allow your CD time and space to get in the mood at his own unhurried pace. Don't take occasional disinterest personally or assume it means you're undesirable.

The CD views physical intimacy as a part of whole-life bonding rather than an end in itself. Help your CD partner connect intimacy to your profound emotional closeness. Exchange meaningful glances, light caresses, and thoughtful verbal affirmations to create an unrushed tone where your CD feels comfortable baring himself completely—in every sense.

Prioritize Physical Connection for MYs

On the flip side, the passionate MY feels cherished mainly through regular physical intimacy. He thrives when his partner initiates romantic gestures like massages, playful touches, steamy make-out sessions, and extended foreplay. For the MY, giving and receiving affection is a top priority, not an afterthought.

The MY sees lovemaking as his most precious bonding time with you when he feels fully immersed in the relationship. Deprivation of physical intimacy makes him feel profoundly unwanted and unloved. If your work and family schedule is hectic, make sure to still pen intimacy into your calendar—just as you would any high-priority item. Protect that one-on-one connection.

Balance Differences with Patience and Effort

Neither approach is right or wrong—the key is balancing your differences. If you're the MY, be patient in allowing your CD partner time to move things forward physically. Don't pressure, pout, or act entitled, which will make him retreat further. If you're the CD, understand your MY partner feels most loved when physical intimacy is constant rather than sporadic. Make concerted efforts to initiate affection since this nourishes your MY partner's sense of belonging. Meet halfway.

Foster Emotional Connections with CDs

Cave Dweller (CD) men, known for their introspective and inward nature, may present themselves as somewhat aloof or may find it challenging to articulate their feelings directly. This can be especially noticeable in the aftermath of disagreements or conflicts. To nurture emotional connections with CDs, it's imperative to cultivate an environment of open communication that feels safe and non-threatening. By approaching your CD partner with a non-judgmental and understanding demeanor, you lay the foundation for deeper emotional interactions. It's essential to radiate empathy and patience, especially if he requires additional time to process and articulate his thoughts before opening up.

For example, after a disagreement, a Cave Dweller may go quiet and want to be alone to process his thoughts. Approaching him repeatedly to discuss the issue right away could make him feel pressured. Give him space for reflection, then calmly check in the next day. Your empathy and patience will provide the safety he needs to open up.

Respond with Patience, Not Criticism

Criticism, impatience, and pressing a CD man repeatedly to respond before he feels ready can lead to withdrawal and hinder emotional intimacy. Responding to his needs with kindness and patience fosters a sense of safety and security, enabling a richer, more authentic emotional connection. It's about allowing the space and freedom for him to express himself genuinely, without the fear of being judged or misunderstood.

Ask Open-Ended Questions

To encourage your CD man to open up about his inner world and thoughts, ask open-ended questions that provide him the opportunity to share more about himself. Explore topics such as his personal beliefs, aspirations, regrets, cherished childhood memories, envisioned future goals, and dreams. Such conversations can serve as windows to his soul, offering glimpses of his deepest thoughts and feelings. After all, the more you know, the more you know to love...

Practice Generous Listening

Active and attentive listening is crucial in these interactions. Avoid interrupting or preparing your response while he is sharing. Instead, reflect on what you heard, seek clarification if needed, and assure him that his thoughts and feelings are valued and appreciated. Provide reassurances like, "I truly appreciate you opening up and sharing that with me," to convey your gratitude and understanding. Such affirmations strengthen the bond and enhance the feeling of being valued and heard.

Plan Low-Pressure Shared Activities

To further deepen emotional intimacy, plan and schedule activities that are relaxing and low-pressure. Opt for activities like stargazing, cooking together, hiking, assembling puzzles, or reading novels side-by-side. Engage in activities that are conducive to sharing and connecting but are also comfortable and pressure-free for your CD partner. These quieter, more serene activities create an environment where CDs can share their deeper thoughts and feelings more comfortably.

Value Companionable Silence

Being content with silence is equally important as engaging in conversation. CDs may find comfort and solace in silence, and respecting this need is crucial in fostering emotional intimacy. By appreciating the silent moments as much as the conversational ones, you create a balanced and harmonious connection.

Invest Time and Patience

The journey to emotional intimacy with a CD man is gradual and requires consistent effort, patience, and understanding. It's about building a trustful environment where vulnerability is embraced and cherished. Much like a plant steadily reaching for sunlight, nurturing emotional intimacy is a deliberate process. It might seem like a massive undertaking at first, but as we persevere, we begin to bask in the warm sunlight of love—and that fuels further growth.

Prioritize Physical Intimacy for MYs

Mountain Yellers stand in contrast to Cave Dwellers when it comes to expressing love and forming connections. Where CDs may find solace in mental and emotional connections, MYs crave the affirmation and warmth found in physical closeness and intimacy. This intimacy is manifested through various expressions such as sex, cuddling, hand-holding, massages, and other forms of tactile gestures. For your MY man, these gestures are not just acts of love but also significant avenues through which he feels deeply connected and cherished.

For example, an MY man may deeply appreciate when his partner initiates intimate touching like massages, kissing, or hand-holding while watching TV together. These loving physical gestures make him feel cared for in his love language.

Provide Physical Connection

MY partners feel most loved and secure when physical intimacy is a woven, seamless element throughout everyday life. They appreciate it when it's not just confined to sporadic, isolated encounters and not always initiated by their partner alone. For them, the act of physical connection is seen as essential bonding time, representing a profound union rather than just fleeting moments of pleasure. It's the silent conversation between souls, the exchange of feelings through touch, that makes the bond stronger and more resilient. So, know you don't need rose petals to make your feelings known.

Be Consistent

To satiate your MY man's primary love language, it's essential to express love through frequent non-sexual physical affection. This could be through daily gestures like back rubs, playing with his hair, embracing him warmly when he returns home from work, waking him with gentle kisses, or holding hands during a movie. These thoughtful, consistent touches are the heartbeat of your relationship with an MY, fulfilling his intrinsic need for physical connection and expression.

Keep the Spark Alive Through Flirting

To keep the flame burning, flirting is key. Send suggestive texts; leave flirty, affectionate notes around for him to find; openly discuss your sexual fantasies; and don't hesitate to compliment and praise his physique. These actions serve as constant reminders of your attraction and desire, reinforcing his sense of being wanted and valued.

Prioritize and Schedule Intimacy

Regular date nights are also pivotal in maintaining physical intimacy. Make time for events or dining out that naturally progress into more intimate encounters. Amid chaotic work and family schedules, it's crucial to proactively prioritize and, if necessary, schedule intimacy. This ensures that your connection doesn't get overshadowed or crowded out by other obligations and responsibilities.

Take the Lead

Initiating intimacy is a powerful way to make your MY partner feel deeply cherished and desired. It's essential not always to be passive or wait for him to make all the advances. By actively seeking to connect physically, you validate his needs and desires, contributing to a more balanced and fulfilled relationship dynamic.

Make Romantic Gestures

Both CDs and MYs report relationships growing stale over time as the intoxication of new love wears off. Counteract this common decline by surprising your partner with thoughtful gestures and making your excitement about the relationship contagious. Experiment to see which kinds of surprises each personality most appreciates.

CD Surprises

Catch your CD off-guard with unexpected moments he will appreciate: pack a gourmet picnic to enjoy together in a secluded meadow, leave a handwritten love letter tucked in his briefcase, compile a playlist encapsulating "our song" memories, cook him a candlelit dinner of his favorite meal unprompted, or secretly book a cozy cabin getaway for just the two of you to escape from routine.

MY Surprises

Appeal to his thirst for spontaneity and adventure. Initiate trying something new and naughty in the bedroom, take a day trip to an amusement park, arrange front-row tickets to see his favorite band in concert, or book an impromptu hot air balloon ride at sunrise. The sky is truly the limit.

No matter how long you've been together, you can reinvent date nights, refresh routines, and plan escapades that make your partner feel adored. Injecting that element of surprise and fun is key to avoiding relationship boredom.

Schedule Date Nights

Between kids, work demands, household chores, and technology distractions, couples often find they've gone weeks without dedicated one-on-one time. But regularly scheduling date nights safeguards your bond. Take turns picking date activities well suited to each of your interests and energy levels.

For homebodies, potential date ideas could include a game night with plush blankets and popcorn, snuggling up to watch a romantic comedy, giving each other massages by candlelight, playing footsie under the table over a gourmet dinner you cooked together, or slow dancing in the living room.

For thrill-seekers, fun date nights out might mean salsa dancing classes, playing mini golf or bowling, visiting a comedy club, attending a concert or pro sports event, or checking out the exhibits at an interactive science museum.

Mix up quiet nights in and lively nights on the town. But carve out a designated couple of times without distractions. Consistency is key, so it doesn't slip through the cracks.

Revisit Relationship Firsts

As years roll on, many long-term couples find themselves looking back at their early days together, a time filled with excitement and a sense of discovery. Intentionally revisiting these memorable, foundational moments can help bring back some of that initial spark and joy, reminding both partners of the love and happiness that marked the beginning of their journey together.

Imagine a cozy night in, just the two of you, with a bowl of fresh popcorn, going through old photo albums and mementos from the days when you just started dating and or got married. Discuss what was going through your minds and your hearts back then, reconnect with those initial emotions, and re-experience the happiness and the laughter of those early days.

Share Significant Milestones

Remember the anniversary of your first date? Why not go back to that special place? Walk around and relive those first sweet moments, recalling the nervous excitement and the joy of discovering each other. Share those fond memories and talk about how it felt to be at the starting point of this beautiful journey.

Recreate Your Early First Dates

Take it a step further and recreate one of your favorite early dates. Recall every detail—the food, the music, the conversations. Read your old love letters and rekindle the romance and the butterflies that came with every word, every shared moment. It's about bringing back the joy and the excitement that was so tangible during those initial days.

Revisit Your Wedding Day

For married couples, revisit your wedding day. Watching your wedding video or going through the photos from your ceremony and reception can bring back the feelings of joy and love that surrounded you as you made those lifelong commitments to each other. It's a beautiful reminder of the promises made and the shared happiness of that day.

Reminisce Over Early Adventures

Think back to the adventures and the shared experiences of your honeymoon or the early travels you had together. Everything was so new and exhilarating. Talk about those shared discoveries, the fun, the laughter, and the joy of exploring the world together. These shared experiences are the building blocks of your relationship, and revisiting them can strengthen your bond more than you might imagine.

By reconnecting with these fond memories and reliving those happy times, you're not just reminiscing about the past but also reinforcing the love and the bond that has grown since then. It provides perspective on how far you've come and reignites the initial charm and excitement, enriching your relationship in the present. It's all too easy to fall into ruts, but focusing on your past adventures will push you to plot out new ones.

Write Old-Fashioned Love Letters

In our fast-paced, digital world, the art of penning a heartfelt love letter seems nearly forgotten, but reviving this intimate tradition can help to convey your deepest feelings. It's a tangible testament to love that surpasses fleeting digital messages, creating enduring tokens of affection.

Whether on holidays or just because, exchange heartfelt letters to express why your love is still blossoming, to reminisce about cherished memories, and to share your excitement for future endeavors and intimate fantasies. Include inside jokes, compliments, and any affectionate sentiments that reflect your unique bond. Each letter becomes a time capsule, too, teeming with love to look back on.

Create a conducive writing environment by lighting candles, playing romantic music, and pouring a glass of wine to help your thoughts flow sincerely and articulate your feelings profoundly. Use quality stationery and careful penmanship to make the letter a visual and tactile experience, and seal it with a lipstick kiss for a personal touch.

Strategically place your heartfelt notes where they'll be discovered unexpectedly, turning an ordinary moment into an extraordinary one. A love letter is a timeless, personal reflection of your feelings, offering a deeper connection with your partner and enriching your relationship with warmth and old-world romance.

Plan Trips and Weekend Getaways

Whisking your man away to a surprise destination can provide a breath of fresh air to your relationship, offering a chance to break from the mundane and rediscover each other along the way. The anticipation, surprise, and fresh environment can spark romance and create lasting memories. Here's how you can pull it off.

Weekend Escapes

Silently arrange a surprise escape to somewhere serene, like a cozy cabin tucked away in a lush forest, a charming beachfront suite with sweeping ocean views, or a quaint bed and breakfast nestled in the countryside. Consider your partner's preferences—maybe they would enjoy a secluded resort where the world feels a million miles away.

Plan a range of activities to relish each other's company: arrange for a couple's massage, plot romantic sunset strolls along the beach, map out scenic hiking trails, and plan lazy mornings with extra cuddle time by a crackling fireplace. A well-thought-out itinerary shows consideration and maximizes the time spent enjoying each other's company in a new setting.

Extended Trips

Delve deeper into your partner's desires and secretly plan the ultimate dream vacation to a destination they've always fantasized about. Or, add an element of adventure by choosing a location neither of you has been to—a city with rich history, a tropical paradise like Bora Bora, or the romantic streets of Paris—allowing you both to explore and create memories in uncharted territories.

To maintain the element of surprise, manage every detail of travel logistics from bookings to packing lists discreetly. Your partner will likely want to pack his own bags, but you can provide a general necessities list without giving away the destination. Then, unveil the meticulously planned mystery location when the bags are packed and the anticipation has reached its peak!

The Unveiling

The big reveal is crucial when it comes to surprise getaways, so consider something novel. Create a scavenger hunt that leads to the destination reveal or simply hand over the tickets at the airport. The moment of revelation can be just as memorable as the trip itself, so give this part the attention it's due.

Bond Over Mutual Interests and Hobbies

Having shared interests and hobbies creates a multitude of possibilities for spending quality time together, which can be a foundational element in sustaining a thriving relationship. Whether it's exploring new activities or diving deeper into each partner's existing hobbies, engaging in shared interests can make your time together more enjoyable and fulfilling.

Take Classes Together

Consider enrolling in a class together. It could be something creative like pottery, painting or something more dynamic like ballroom dance. Engaging in wine tasting, archery, or cooking lessons can also offer a fun and exciting way to discover new hobbies together, giving you both the chance to bond over shared experiences and maybe even discover a newfound passion.

Stay Active Together

Staying active is also an excellent way to spend time together. Whether it's joining a running club, exploring nature trails by biking or hiking, or learning paddle boarding, engaging in cardiovascular activities not only benefits your health but also gives an extra layer of connection through shared goals and achievements. These active pursuits can energize your relationship and offer numerous opportunities for creating lasting memories.

Adopt a Pet

If both of you have a soft spot for animals, consider adopting a pet. Bringing a puppy or a kitten into your lives can add a new dimension to your relationship as you both share in caring for your new furry family member. It's a shared responsibility that can bring joy and a sense of shared purpose.

Get Your Nerd On

For those with a penchant for more intellectual pursuits, you could find common ground in nerdy interests—a term, here, used with utmost endearment. Dive into the world of video or board games, attend conventions like Comic-Con together, indulge in cosplay, build computers, or get involved in fantasy football. Engaging in such activities is not only fun but also opens avenues for learning more about each other's preferences and skills.

Take on DIY Projects Together

If you're both hands-on, try engaging in DIY projects. Remodeling a part of your house, woodworking, indulging in gardening, or acquiring new home repair skills can be both productive and bonding experiences. It's about teamwork and creating something meaningful together.

Strengthen Your Connection

Through bonding over mutual interests and shared activities, you create a plethora of inside jokes, shared stories, and engaging debates. It brings a deeper connection, understanding, and a unique layer of physical chemistry, especially through activities that involve physical engagement. This shared time makes your relationship more layered, filled with joy, fun, and shared achievements.

These shared pursuits and adventures offer a well-rounded approach to building and maintaining a lively and fulfilling relationship, ensuring that the connection between you remains strong. It shouldn't always be, "How was your day?" What you want to say is, "What a day that was we had together."

Discuss Needs and Desires

Opening the dialogue about desires and needs is crucial, especially for long-standing partners. It's all too common for couples to sidestep frank discussions about their wants and hopes, leaving too much to assumption and silent expectation. An unaddressed wish or a silent hope can lead to lingering hurts and silent rejections, so it's pivotal to break through the barriers of assumption and hope to delve into proactive, compassionate conversations about each other's needs and desires, thus avoiding the pitfalls of miscommunication.

Break Through Assumption Barriers

Understanding and sharing your interpretations of both physical and emotional closeness can be enlightening. It's beneficial to discover whether your ideals align or diverge and to discuss these topics openly, without defensiveness or prejudice. Analyzing the daily factors that either enhance or impair your connection is equally critical. Collaborative brainstorming for compromises can illuminate the path forward.

Use Quizzes to Spark Insight

Taking quizzes like MojoUpgrade or LoveLanguages together can be a helpful tool to reflect on mutual areas and pinpoint gaps in preferences, opening the door to understanding and revealing overlaps and variations in desires. It's important to examine your views on exclusivity and contentment in the relationship and to consider whether attitudes and feelings have changed over time. Quizzes will often ask questions that we wouldn't be able to pose ourselves, so avail yourself of these resources, and have some fun while you're at it.

Reveal Desires Without Shame

Sharing fantasies, desires, or requests without judgment or shame can lead to exploring intriguing possibilities together. It's essential to identify the unique pleasures and stress points in your relationship and to discuss the steps each partner could take to make the other feel more cherished and supported. Expressing appreciation for your partner's efforts can lead to a deeper understanding and mutual growth.

Maintain Open Communication

Maintaining open dialogue around desires and needs is essential, as it reminds you both that a partner's inner world is not an open book without asking. Frequent exchange of perspectives can prevent misunderstandings from simmering and underscore the importance of not assuming to know each other's deepest thoughts and desires without explicit communication.

Key Takeaways

The essence of this chapter has been nurturing and cherishing each other's unique language of love, regardless of differing personal inclinations and preferences. Let's take a look at what we've discussed, as you now consider the applications...

- **Shut Down Fear and Open Up:** It's not just about sharing thoughts; it's about creating a space of trust and non-judgment. It's vital to articulate feelings and desires calmly, avoiding the accumulation of unspoken hurts and assumptions.

- **Understand and Appreciate:** Delving deeper to truly understand and acknowledge each other's unique desires and needs is foundational. It's about cultivating an environment where appreciation is expressed and felt consistently.

- **Compromise and Engage:** Finding a middle ground and actively participating in mutual interests is key. It's about creating shared experiences and memories, promoting mutual satisfaction and joy.

- **Detail Desires:** Unveiling your deepest desires and fantasies without fear or shame allows the relationship to explore new dimensions. You can't expect your man to be a mind-reader. Ask and you may just receive.

- **Prioritize and Cherish:** Investing time in each other through shared activities and thoughtful gestures is essential. It's about keeping the flame alive and maintaining a strong connection amidst the daily routines of life.

- **Embrace Differences:** Understanding, embracing, and respecting each other's unique needs and preferences is pivotal in building a harmonious, fulfilling relationship. It's all about mutual growth and understanding that fortifies the relationship over time.

- **Reflect Regularly:** Regularly take time to understand and meet each other's needs. This strengthens your bond continuously.

By deploying these insights and strategies, you pave the way to a deeper, more fulfilling relationship. Be assured: this will take time—and the work is never really done—but thankfully, the process itself is a pleasure, so set forth with joy.

Chapter Four

Balancing Social Needs

Balancing social needs in a relationship is often a pivotal point, especially when one partner prefers solitude and the other is more inclined toward social engagements. In this chapter, we'll focus on finding a middle ground between a CD's need for alone time and an MY's preference for being around people. We'll address how to understand, respect, and cater to each other's needs, ensuring that both partners feel valued.

When one partner seeks solitude and the other thrives in social gatherings, it's about merging two different worlds effectively. It's not just about setting boundaries or planning activities; it's about being open, understanding, and willing to experience each other's worlds. It's learning to value both solitude and interaction, creating a relationship where both can be enjoyed equally.

Harmonize a CD's Need for Solitude with an MY's Social Inclinations

In every relationship, the act of balancing disparate needs and desires stands as a cornerstone of unity. Achieving equilibrium isn't just about compromise; it's about sculpting a shared existence where individual needs—periodic solitude for CDs and frequent social interactions for MYs—are both celebrated and respected, laying the foundations for a nurturing and loving environment.

Understanding your partner's individuality is key. For instance, after a demanding week, a CD man might crave a quiet evening at home, engrossed in a book or a solo hobby. Contrastingly, an MY man might be energized by the idea of hosting a barbecue with friends or heading out to a live game. Balancing these inclinations requires thoughtful planning and communication. Maybe it's about designating certain evenings for personal downtime and others for social events. Or perhaps it's about finding middle ground, like attending a small gathering or planning a date night just for the two of you. By actively acknowledging and accommodating these tendencies, the relationship gains depth, cultivating a space where both partners feel heard and valued. Do you want to be heard? Then listen. It's called The Golden Rule for a reason.

Plan Activities That Cater to Both Personalities

When you're trying to plan activities in a relationship, it's extremely important to think about what both partners enjoy. We're looking to find those shared moments that can make both individuals happy, whether it's a quiet night that a CD might enjoy or a busy gathering that an MY might love. This means creating a shared space that respects and values each person's unique needs and preferences.

Make Both Partners Feel Valued

Though easier said than done, of course, ensuring that both partners' needs are addressed should always be the goal. Consider this scenario: Tom, an MY, loves cycling and often spends his weekends on long biking trails. His partner, a CD named Sally, prefers sketching landscapes in the park. Instead of seeing these preferences as opposing forces, they strike a balance. Tom might choose a scenic trail where, after a fulfilling ride, he joins Alex for an hour of quiet reflection and sketching.

It's not about one partner yielding to the other but about finding creative ways to integrate their passions.

Gradually Introduce CDs to Intimate Social Settings

Fusing contrasting social preferences requires a delicate approach, especially when aligning the quieter disposition of a CD with more engaging settings. CDs often cherish solitude and intimate interactions, and a gradual introduction to more lively social scenes is crucial to prevent them from feeling overwhelmed. The incorporation of CDs into dynamic environments necessitates understanding, patience, and a balanced approach to meeting in the middle.

Start with Small, Familiar Gatherings

Start by involving CDs in smaller, more intimate gatherings, where the ambiance is relaxed, and the crowd is familiar. This approach offers them an opportunity to acclimate to social settings without feeling cornered or overwhelmed. By providing them with a secure and comforting environment, CDs can slowly extend their comfort zones, embrace new experiences, and find enjoyment in social interactions.

Be Attentive to Comfort Levels

It's also crucial to be attentive to CDs' preferences and comfort levels, considering their viewpoints when planning gatherings and allowing them the flexibility to retreat if they choose to. Check in with your partner periodically, and if they've reached their limit, help out with a sound escape-hatch excuse.

Communicate Your Expectations

Moreover, communication plays a pivotal role in this harmonization process. Discussing expectations, establishing boundaries, and sharing experiences contribute to developing a nurturing environment where both partners feel heard and understood. By learning about each other's needs and respecting individual comforts, a stronger bond is formed, enhancing the relationship's resilience and longevity. Before venturing out, discuss how long you intend to stay at a gathering, for instance. Will you split off or stick together? Planning ahead will always help to make for smooth social outings.

Appreciate MY's Need for Broader Social Engagements

On the flip side of the social spectrum, MYs crave broader social engagements and thrive on interactions with diverse groups of people. Acknowledging and appreciating these needs is integral to nurturing a balanced and fulfilling relationship. MYs draw energy and joy from being around others, engaging in lively conversations, and participating in frequent social activities. Recognizing this intrinsic need is essential for cultivating mutual respect and understanding within the relationship.

Allow Freedom to Explore and Discover

MYs find fulfillment in exploring different social landscapes, meeting new people, and immersing themselves in varied experiences. While they cherish their time with their CD partners, having the freedom to engage in broader social interactions is vital for their well-being and happiness. Balancing this need with the relationship's demands requires open communication, compromise, and mutual respect.

Establish Open Dialogue

To nurture balance, establishing an open dialogue about each partner's social needs and desires is crucial. Finding the right setting and time for these discussions is equally important. Perhaps it's during a quiet dinner at home, a walk in the park, or even while running simple errands together. The key is choosing moments free from distractions, allowing both partners to be fully present

Respect Contrasting Social Dispositions

Viewing a partner's different social style as a personal affront can lead to unnecessary tension. Instead, it's academically and psychologically sound to approach these differences with an analytical mindset. Recognize them as distinct personality traits rather than comparative judgments.

Moreover, showing respect for your partner's disposition can set a positive precedent. When one partner exhibits understanding and

Set Boundaries for Personal Space and Time

Boundaries serve as the essential invisible lines drawn around our personal space and time, acting as silent protectors of our well-being and peace of mind. Their implementation and respect are critical in nurturing a healthy, thriving relationship, especially when one involves individuals with varying social needs and preferences.

Respect His Personal Time

For CDs, who lean toward solitude, personal time isn't a mere preference; it's a fundamental need, a sanctuary for recharging and self-reflection. This aspect of their personality, when misunderstood, can often lead to misconceptions or feelings of being sidelined in a relationship.

Consider the scenario of Robert, a dedicated CD, who works in a bustling office environment. After long hours of constant (often unwanted) interaction, he yearns for an evening immersed in a good book or playing a solo instrument. His partner, more extroverted, might interpret this as Robert distancing himself. In reality, it's Robert's way of rejuvenating to be a better partner in the relationship.

Do:

- Acknowledge and Accept: Recognize your man's need for alone time without taking it personally.

- Communicate: Discuss and understand how each partner values and uses free time.

- Schedule: If needed, establish shared time and personal time slots to avoid clashes.

Don't:

- Intrude: Avoid constantly interrupting or trying to participate in your man's solitude activities unless invited.

- Make Assumptions: Do not equate your partner's need for personal time with a lack of interest in the relationship.

- Compare: Avoid comparing his use of free time with how others, like friends or family, spend theirs. Each individual's needs are unique.

By fostering understanding and respect for these personal space needs, relationships can strike a balance where both partners feel validated and content.

Engage in Joint Classes or Workshops

Embarking on joint activities like classes or workshops serves as a meaningful avenue for partners to bond, explore, and create shared memories and experiences.

From a psychological standpoint, learning together can be particularly impactful. Engaging in a shared learning environment allows both you and your man to tackle new challenges collaboratively, thereby promoting mutual problem-solving and adaptability. When you're both exposed to new information, you're more likely to discuss, debate, and reinforce what you've learned, which aids retention and creates a shared intellectual foundation. This joint cognitive effort can result in a stronger bond, as it forces both partners to see, understand, and appreciate the other's perspective in real-time. It's less about the content of what's being learned, and more about the collaborative process and the mutual understanding that ensues.

Ensure Mutual Comfort

When engaging in activities, especially when the relationship consists of partners with differing social inclinations, the chosen activity must align with both partners' comfort and interest levels. Be it a serene and focused painting class or an interactive, bustling cooking workshop, the essence is to ensure enjoyment and comfort for both parties. If you have to twist your partner's arm, it's likely you're taking the wrong approach.

Allow Separate Nights Out with Friends

Understanding and appreciating each person's need for individual time and space is an integral part of a healthy relationship. By encouraging each other to spend time with their respective friends, couples reinforce mutual respect and acknowledge each other's independent lives and personal friendships. This autonomy is not indicative of distance but is instead a healthy practice that nourishes and fortifies the relationship.

Common Issues and How to Mitigate Them

- **Jealousy:**

Issue: One partner feels left out or threatened by the other's interactions with friends.

Mitigation: Open a line of communication. Discuss the root of the jealousy and reassure each other of your commitment. Consider occasional joint outings to foster familiarity among both partners' circles of friends.

- **Overstepping Boundaries:**

Issue: One partner feels their nights out are being monitored or controlled.

Mitigation: Set clear and mutual boundaries. Understand that everyone needs personal space, and respect each other's freedom.

- **Miscommunication:**

Issue: Confusion or misinterpretation regarding the frequency or nature of nights out.

Mitigation: Regularly check in with each other. Having a clear understanding of each other's plans ensures that there are no surprises and both are on the same page.

- **Neglect:**

Issue: One partner feels neglected or that their needs aren't being prioritized.

Mitigation: Balance is key. While spending time with friends is important, it's crucial to also allocate quality time for the relationship itself. Ensure you're both satisfied with the time shared together.

Addressing these issues preemptively through understanding and open dialogue can prevent misunderstandings and bolster the trust and respect foundational to any relationship.

Host Mutual Social Events or Gatherings

Planning and hosting social events or gatherings is a significant aspect of building a shared life. It provides an opportunity for couples to create collective memories and present a united front within their social circles. It's a convergence of different friends and family, integrating varying aspects of each partner's life.

For instance, a couple may decide to host a holiday party and invite friends from their respective social groups. The MY partner enjoys mingling with guests while the CD partner feels most comfortable preparing food and making sure everything is running smoothly. They work as a team to create an event celebrating their love while also accommodating both partners' comfort levels.

When organizing such events, both partners need to collaborate and incorporate elements that reflect their individual preferences and personalities. Whether it's an intimate gathering or a larger celebration, the event should be a representation of both partners' identities. One thing is certain: Things tend to work out when you work together as one.

Collaborate in Decision-Making

Following up on the above, both partners must be involved in making decisions regarding the guest list, menu, and overall setup. Have a penchant for taking over? Consider allocating these jobs to your man to make him feel more involved:

Music Maestro

Entrust him with creating the event's playlist. Not only does music set the tone, but it's a fantastic way for him to express his tastes and contribute to the ambiance.

Beverage Boss

Let him take the lead in selecting and mixing drinks, whether it's choosing wines and beers or crafting signature cocktails. It's a blend of art and science, and it adds a personal touch to the festivities.

Tech Troubleshooter

If there's any tech involved, like setting up speakers or managing lighting, let him be in charge. It ensures smooth operation and takes one more thing off the list.

Seating Strategist

Allow him to decide on the seating arrangements. It's a subtle way of ensuring everyone feels comfortable and can make for interesting dinner conversations based on his insights.

Theme Thinker

If the event has a theme, let him brainstorm and help execute the idea. Whether it's decor, attire, or games related to the theme, his input can bring a fresh perspective.

By giving him these roles, not only does it promote collaborative planning, but it also ensures both partners feel valued and integral to the event's success.

Establish Meaningful Traditions

Hosting gatherings with regularity can establish a sense of tradition, which often proves powerful. Consider the many reasons why this proves a powerful force:

- **Stability and Predictability:** Regular traditions can offer a sense of stability and predictability in a relationship. These consistent events act as anchor points, providing moments of joint planning and anticipation.

- **Shared History:** Over time, recurring events contribute to a collective narrative. Each tradition-infused event becomes a chapter in a shared history.

- **Collaborative Skills:** The act of planning and executing traditional events enhances cooperative skills. It requires joint decision-making, playing to each partner's strengths, and managing any arising challenges together.

- **Reinforcing Commitment:** Regularly upheld traditions serve as a testament to the commitment and effort both partners are investing in the relationship. It's a tangible representation of prioritizing the relationship and each other.

- **Enhanced Communication:** The planning and feedback phases associated with these traditions necessitate open dialogue. It offers opportunities for both partners to express their preferences, expectations, and any reservations.

- **Deepened Connection:** Engaging in traditions fosters a deeper connection by creating unique experiences that are exclusive to the relationship, differentiating it from other social interactions.

In a nutshell, traditions in hosting not only infuse events with significance but also play a pivotal role in strengthening the relational fabric between partners.

Celebrate Milestones Together

Recognizing milestones within a relationship is essential for sustaining unity. Such milestones—comprising personal achievements, anniversaries, or joint endeavors—act as markers in a couple's shared journey, denoting mutual experiences and progress. By consciously marking these occasions, couples can evaluate their shared history, focusing on past experiences, faced challenges, and mutual achievements. For example, when a partner completes a significant task, such as graduate school, the celebration can extend beyond the achievement itself to encompass the supportive roles both played throughout the process.

Strengthen Your Bond

Celebrations are more than traditions; they're acknowledgments of the journey a couple has undertaken together. These events highlight growth, challenges faced, and moments of unity. They provide a moment to value each other's contributions and reflect on shared memories. Often, there's a misconception that men prefer to continue without acknowledgment or praise. This is very much a myth. Recognizing your man's achievements and regularly expressing gratitude can significantly boost his morale and enhance the quality of the relationship. What better way to acknowledge something than with a proper party?

Create Shared Memories

It's crucial to set aside these moments, no matter how big or small, to acknowledge and appreciate the shared path you've walked on together. By actively participating in celebrating these milestones, couples cultivate a reservoir of shared memories and experiences, enhancing the unity and mutual respect that serve as the pillars of the relationship. It's about intentionally creating space to make each other feel valued and cherished and about manifesting lasting memories. The act of celebrating becomes a mirror, reflecting the enduring commitment, love, and mutual understanding that are the lifeblood of the relationship. It's a gentle reminder of the accumulated strength, the woven resilience, and the shared journey.

Recognize Individual Achievements in Social Groups

Recognizing each other's achievements in social settings is paramount. When partners demonstrate their pride and appreciation for each other's achievements within their social circles, it becomes a vibrant illustration of the intrinsic support and respect embedded within the relationship. Consider the following ways in which to showcase support for your man:

- **Public Compliments:** Praise him in front of friends and family when he achieves something, even if it's a small accomplishment.

- **Toast to Success:** At a dinner or gathering, raise a toast to his achievements or milestones, whether they are personal or professional.

- **Share Stories:** Narrate instances where he overcame challenges or displayed exceptional skills, especially if those listening aren't privy to the details.

- **Social Media Shout-outs:** A post recognizing his accomplishments or simply expressing gratitude for his support can be both personal and public.

- **Include Him in Conversations:** If discussions revolve around a topic he's knowledgeable about or has recently achieved something in, steer the conversation his way.

- **Acknowledge Joint Ventures:** If you've achieved something together, emphasize the importance of his role in that success when discussing it.

- **Display Physical Affection:** In the right context, a simple gesture like holding his hand or a pat on the back can convey pride and support without words.

- **Gifts:** Presenting him with a thoughtful gift in front of close friends or family can be a public recognition of his personal or professional milestones.

- **Seek His Opinion:** In group settings, ask for his insights or perspectives, particularly in areas he excels in.

- **Photo Displays:** Showcase pictures at home capturing moments of his achievements, ensuring they're visible during gatherings or events.

Key Takeaways

Balancing the interplay between solitude and sociability is foundational in a harmonious relationship. Navigating between a CD's need for solitude and an MY's social inclinations is vital for creating an environment of mutual respect and growth.

- **Know His Needs (And Make Yours Known):** Acknowledge and harmonize the needs for solitude and social interactions to build a better relationship.

- **Plan Inclusively:** Develop inclusive activities that resonate with both partners, making each feel valued and acknowledged. Don't force him to do things to which he's opposed, but do look for compromises and ways to share your own interests.

- **Broadcast Boundaries:** Clearly defined and respected personal boundaries are crucial for maintaining harmony and individual well-being within the relationship.

- **Learn to Learn as One:** Engage in joint learning experiences to enhance mutual understanding and deepen your connection. Teach each other. Be taught together. You'll learn to love in newfangled ways.

- **Respect Social Needs:** Respect and appreciate separate social engagements to fortify the relationship and bring in fresh perspectives.

- **Host Shared Social Events:** Hosting events creates a platform for shared interests and meaningful social interactions, enhancing the relationship's social texture.

- **Celebrate Milestones Together:** Acknowledging and celebrating shared milestones reinforce mutual respect, shared joy, and the collective journey.

- **Recognize His Achievements:** Recognizing your man's achievements in social groups fortifies mutual respect and showcases shared pride in the relationship.

In the realm of sociology and relationship dynamics, a central tenet emerges: relationships thrive not just on individual growth, but on the confluence of two distinct social narratives. Understanding and accommodating each other's social needs is not a mere nicety; it's an essential aspect of a well-balanced partnership.

Navigating the complexities of these social needs goes beyond mere compromise. It's an exercise in understanding the underlying influences that shape a person's interactions, desires, and boundaries.

Embracing this concept helps couples create a richer, more nuanced connection. It's an exploration—a joint academic endeavor, if you will—where both partners become students of each other's social landscapes.

If you love your man, you'll want him to have a happy social life, so get involved and help him to build one!

Chapter Five

Emotional Harmony

When a person has emotional harmony, they can maintain inner peace despite the ups and downs of everyday life. To achieve emotional harmony, it's crucial for a person to practice positive self-talk and focus on what they can control in their life, rather than what they can't.

Positive self-talk is when a person's internal dialogue helps them feel good about themselves, enabling them to feel and behave at their best both for themselves and for others, including their partner. Examples of positive self-talk include affirmations like: "I am enough," "I deserve to be happy," and "I deserve to have great health." One simple way to practice positive self-talk is by posting sticky notes on your bathroom mirror and reading them each time you see them.

A simple way to figure out what you can control in your life is to create a list. You can also draw a circle and fill it in with things that you can control in your life, then draw a surrounding circle and fill it in with things that you can't control in your life.

For example, some things within your control in life include your self-talk, attitude, effort, schedule, diet, fitness, self-care, and even your breathing. While some aspects of life are within your control, there are also factors that remain beyond your control, including other people's actions, their feelings, whether people like or dislike you, the weather, the passing of time, and the future.

Similarly, when a couple experiences emotional harmony in a relationship, they can maintain inner peace despite any ups and downs they might experience. Positive self-talk and focusing on what can and can't be controlled are just as important in a relationship as it is in someone's personal life.

Affirmations can also be used in a relationship. For example, try taking turns writing affirmations on the fridge. Each time both of you are in the kitchen, take a moment to read one of your partner's affirmations aloud, and have them do the same for you.

Establishing what can and can't be controlled in a relationship can also be achieved by creating a list. The "circle" method can be used by both parties, too, to figure out what can and can't be controlled in the relationship.

In your relationship, there are things within your control, such as how you treat your partner, how you communicate with them, the level of assistance you provide, and setting boundaries. However, there are some aspects of your relationship that remain beyond your control, including your partner's actions, their feelings, their time, their relationships with friends and family, their goals, and the future of your relationship.

Part of an emotionally harmonious relationship entails being willing to understand and listen to your partner's emotions. Understanding your partner's emotions doesn't mean that you have to agree with everything they say, it simply means that you try your best to understand and listen to where your partner is coming from.

In this chapter, we'll celebrate the unique emotional strengths that each of you offers, explain how to provide emotional support to MYs in their social endeavors, and encourage the understanding of CDs in their introspective moments. We'll also learn how to navigate vulnerabilities together and gain emotional insights through books, media, and podcasts.

Celebrate the Unique Emotional Strengths You Each Offer

It's important to understand how your partner expresses their emotions. CD men tend to internally reflect on their emotions before they share them, whereas MY men tend to readily share their emotions externally.

CD men tend to express their feelings in a more intentional way, and although it might take them longer to share their emotions, they will do so when they're comfortable. For example, CD men are more likely to choose a select few people to open up to, but once you're in their circle, you have their trust. They're also more comfortable expressing themselves in smaller settings and having deeper conversations. CD men tend to have limited energy when it comes to relationships, so they have to be more selective about who they share their world with.

If you ask CD men about their feelings, they're often more willing to open up and discuss them. Additionally, it's very important to listen to a CD man, inquire about their inner world, and give them space. Moreover, CD men are often more at ease expressing their emotions online, as well as through writing, music, and art.

MY men, on the other hand, tend to be more comfortable verbally expressing their emotions and will share these emotions more quickly.

In fact, MY men tend to work through their emotions by discussing them. However, MY men often pay little attention to their inner needs. For instance, when an MY man feels lonely, he may dismiss it because he's rarely alone.

MY men often possess strong social skills, have a large circle of friends, are comfortable in large groups, and readily engage in small talk.

To celebrate a CD man's emotional strengths, it's important to be patient and understand that it will take time for him to open up emotionally. It's also important to understand that CD men are quiet at times, even with their partners. It doesn't mean that anything is wrong; it just means that they're inwardly focused.

To celebrate a MY man's emotional strengths, it's important to allow them to vent periodically, as MY men tend to work through their emotions by talking. Therefore, it's crucial for an MY man to have a partner who is willing to listen as well as understand that they tend to talk to just about everyone.

Efforts to understand how your partner expresses their emotions can significantly contribute to harmony in your relationship.

Offer Emotional Support to MYs in Their Social Endeavors

Since MY men tend to strike up conversations with anyone, from the cashier at the grocery store to the stranger sitting beside them on an airplane, it's important for their partner to realize that MY men aren't flirting, they simply enjoy engaging in small talk. In fact, whenever an MY man leaves the house, it's common for them to meet people wherever they go.

Given the inclination of MY men to socialize in large groups, it's crucial for them to have a partner who is willing to accompany them to at least some of these parties and social events as well as give them space to attend parties and social events on their own. MY men are often referred to as "the life of the party" because they're typically outgoing, talkative, and energetic. Parties and social gatherings are particularly important for MY men as this is where they recharge. In fact, if they were characters in a video game where hearts symbolized their life force, their hearts would be fully replenished after a night out on the town.

Additionally, an MY man might appreciate surprise parties or impromptu get-togethers with their friends and family. MY men often enjoy activities such as karaoke nights, where they can take center stage, as well as music festivals, cooking classes, wine tastings, escape rooms, dancing classes, sports, trivia nights, open mic nights, improv comedy, and paintball.

On the flip side, if you prefer quiet evenings at home, it's essential to communicate this to your MY partner and plan nights just for the two of you. Or you can always compromise and host a low-key games night with friends, a barbeque, or an intimate dinner party.

Encourage and Understand CDs in Their Introspective Moments

On the other hand, CD men often don't enjoy small talk because they prefer engaging in deeper conversations. Additionally, CD men often find that small talk is boring, drains their energy, and is inauthentic and an overall waste of time.

CD men tend to shy away from large parties and social gatherings, so it's crucial for them to have a partner who is willing to spend some quiet evenings at home. Large parties and social gatherings are especially draining for CD men. In fact, if they were characters in a video game where hearts symbolized their life force, their hearts would be completely depleted by the end of a night out on the town.

Since introverts need time alone to think, especially after working all day with people or after a social event, it's important to give them space, because being alone is what re-energizes them. This doesn't mean that CD men don't want to spend time with their partner, it's simply what they need to be their best selves. Men with a CD personality tend to thrive in peaceful environments that allow for privacy and introspection.

CD men often enjoy going out to restaurants and bars but prefer to go during weekdays when restaurants and bars are less crowded. Other activities that CD men often enjoy include taking a drive, hiking, bike rides, checking out bookstores, going to small breweries, attending drive-in movie theaters where they can enjoy a movie from the comfort of their own vehicle, star gazing, and visiting museums.

In addition, there are plenty of fun things to do at home that CD men might enjoy including watching a movie, playing card and board games, cooking and eating dinner together, enjoying a wine, beer, or liquor tasting at home, and much more.

Navigate Vulnerabilities Together

To build a trusting, honest, and authentic relationship, it's crucial for people to open up and share their vulnerable side with their partner.

Moreover, when partners lower their emotional walls, they can form a closer bond.

It's natural for partners to hide their imperfections and anxieties in the initial stages of a relationship. However, as the relationship develops, it's important to trust your partner and let them in by sharing your vulnerabilities with them.

MY men tend to be more open and willing to share their thoughts and feelings, whereas CD men are often quieter and more private.

However, there are ways to encourage CD men (or MY men if they are having difficulty opening up) to open up and share their vulnerable side. One way is to start talking about your own thoughts and feelings, which might encourage your partner to do the same. And when they do open up, make sure to listen to what they have to say without interrupting.

Gain Emotional Insights through Books, Movies, and Podcasts

Watching movies and TV shows, reading books, and listening to podcasts with your partner are all ways to gain emotional insights from each other.

By mutually choosing relationship-focused literature together, you'll be able to have conversations about your feelings and experiences. To strengthen your relationship, talk about the narratives, approaches to communication, or real-world examples in these books that speak to your respective histories, philosophies, emotional sensitivities, and potential growth areas.

Books that CD men may enjoy include: Quiet: The Power of Introverts in a World That Can't Stop Talking by Susan Cain, How to Be Highly Effective as an Introvert: Communicate, Become A Leader, Influence, and Win Friends by David Inglem, and Hack Your Introvert: You Don't Have to Be an Extrovert to Have the Best Conversations by Grace Malcolm.

Unfortunately, there aren't many books written solely about extroverts, but books that both CD men and MY men may enjoy are The Genius of Opposites: How Introverts and Extroverts Achieve Extraordinary Results Together by Jennifer B. Kahnweiler and The Power of Personality: How Introverts and Extroverts Can Combine to Amazing Effect by Sylvia Loehken.

Watching movies and TV shows that explore various types of relationships can be both fun and enlightening. These visual stories give us a window into different attachment styles, personalities, and ways people communicate. To dig a little deeper and gain some real relationship wisdom, it's useful to hit the pause button and have a chat with your partner about how these fictional tales might relate to your own love life. You can each share what you've learned and any advice you've picked up along the way.

Playing fun and lighthearted games, like online personality and relationship quizzes, can offer a fresh perspective on each other. It's fascinating and eye-opening to explore how your personality types interact and how your needs align or differ. By uncovering each other's primary emotional requirements and love languages, this exploration empowers you to craft a thoughtful plan for nurturing the unique blend of your relationship.

Another valuable tool for enhancing your relationship is reading biographies, autobiographies, and memoirs. There are learning opportunities in discovering the stories of individuals who have adeptly navigated relationship challenges or demonstrated emotional intelligence and effective communication in their own relationships. Discussing the principles and lessons that can be gleaned from their experiences deepens your connection and provides insights into healing.

Staying updated with the latest research-based articles by renowned psychologists, therapists, and marriage counselors can also be beneficial. These resources often cover a wide range of topics, from gender differences and attachment theory to emotional needs and other factors that influence relationships. Engaging in discussions and analysis of this content together ensures that both of you not only grasp it but also relate it to your shared experiences.

Listening to sermons and podcasts that explore spiritual and psychological insights on maintaining healthy relationships can also offer fresh perspectives. Gaining new insights and promoting personal growth can come from tuning into discussions about fostering emotional well-being, effective communication, and healing from past traumas.

You are creating a learning atmosphere that is supportive of mutual growth and understanding by devoting time to these kinds of materials and activities, in addition to serving as mirrors reflecting each other's thoughts and emotions. This deliberate search of information and comprehension gives you both the means to develop your emotional intelligence, conflict resolution abilities, and self-awareness. Engaging with these various media together not only facilitates consuming new information but also enables growing and becoming closer as a couple by cultivating a deeper and wiser bond.

Key Takeaways

Emotional harmony is crucial for maintaining healthy relationships, both with yourself and with your partner. When you experience emotional harmony, you can maintain inner peace despite the ups and downs of everyday life. Likewise, when a couple experiences emotional harmony, they can sustain peace within their relationship, even in the face of life's challenges. Here are a couple of important things to keep in mind:

- **Honor Differences:** Efforts to understand how your partner expresses their emotions can significantly contribute to harmony in your relationship.

- **Support Companionship:** Whether your partner craves quality time and companionship like the MY, or seeks introspective solitude like the CD, make a conscious effort to support them by scheduling moments that cater to their emotional well-being.

- **Seek Understanding:** Create a peaceful environment and respect your CD partner's need for privacy and introspection. Show understanding and encouragement during these moments. This approach fosters a deeper sense of respect and connection in your relationship.

- **Accept Vulnerability:** To build a trusting, honest, and authentic relationship, it's crucial for people to open up and share their vulnerable side with their partner.

- **Embrace Lifelong Learning:** Explore podcasts, watch movies, and read books about relationships as a couple. Discuss the insights you gain to enhance your emotional intelligence and awareness, strengthening your relationship in the process.

- **Cherish Diversity:** It's important to value each other's unique qualities. Recognize how your differences can actually enhance your connection and understanding of each other.

- **Pursue Growth Together:** Encourage personal growth and development for both of you. Acknowledge each other's realizations and insights as steps toward a more meaningful and rewarding partnership.

Remember that this journey is ongoing. Approach it with courage, empathy, and a keen emotional awareness. There's boundless beauty waiting to be uncovered in the growth of your relationship. So, keep moving forward with an open heart and an open mind, and cherish the ever-evolving bond you share.

Chapter Six

Financial Balance

It's important to have a partner who is compatible with you and whose values, goals, and visions align with yours. Financial compatibility is a crucial part of compatibility in a relationship.

Discussing finances with your partner may not be easy, but it's necessary for a stable relationship. It's preferable to have these conversations within the first few months, although financial matters may come up sooner. For instance, going out to dinner is common on a first date, and when the check arrives you have a few options: splitting the bill, offering to pay for the entire bill, or allowing your date to pay for the entire bill. To make a first date less awkward, you could ask this question in advance, either over the phone or through text messages.

To make the topic of money more approachable, you can ask lighthearted questions that provide insight into the other person's relationship with money. For example, you could inquire if they are saving for something special, like a car or a trip.

Other financial areas to explore as you get to know your partner include: budgeting, student loan debt, credit card debt, savings, credit score, retirement plans, and more.

On this financial journey, what really matters is understanding, trust, and working as a team. When we put respect first and work together to figure out our finances, we can make sure everything runs smoothly and peacefully.

Healthily Navigate Financial Disagreements

Because of varying backgrounds, childhood money experiences, and unique personalities, disagreements about finances are common in committed relationships, particularly once the honeymoon phase has passed. For instance, if your partner has a careful and cautious CD personality, they might be concerned and cautious regarding money, spending, and investments. Meanwhile, someone with the adventurous and free-spirited MY personality might prefer making quick decisions without much planning, especially when it comes to finances.

However, despite your different financial outlooks, there are ways to avoid arguments. For example, one of you may prioritize long-term financial goals like savings and investments, while the other may focus on day-to-day spending. Alternatively, both of you can participate in present and future planning. This could be done by designating a day each month to pay bills, review expenses, and manage savings.

If you find yourselves arguing about finances and the conversation becomes unproductive, take a break and revisit it later.

Embracing Different Financial Perspectives

How you're brought up to think about finances has a lasting impact on your later life. For instance, your parents might have instilled budgeting habits by buying generic food brands at the grocery store and sticking to only the essential items on their list. As a result, you might also adopt budget-conscious habits. On the other hand, if your parents shunned grocery lists and opted for name brands, you might do the same. Alternatively, if your parents went grocery shopping on their own, you might not have a reference point for what to buy at the grocery store or how to budget your food shopping.

Also, if your parents discussed finances with you, you may find it more comfortable talking about finances with your partner than if finances were never discussed in your childhood.

In addition, MY men tend to spend more and prioritize social status, whereas CD men often prefer saving their money.

If you and your partner have different financial perspectives, disagreements are likely to arise, potentially leading to arguments about budgeting, significant purchases, and saving for the future. However, if couples focus on compromise and communicate calmly and respectfully using constructive language rather than accusatory statements, disagreements will become less frequent.

It's also valuable to avoid viewing finances in rigid, black-and-white terms. Instead of painting one partner as reckless and the other as overly strict, recognize that both of you ultimately seek financial security. You just have different approaches to achieving it. When you can genuinely understand and empathize with your partner's point of view, you're more likely to find a middle ground.

Another crucial strategy is to be selective about the financial battles you pick. Not every money-related decision needs to escalate into a major debate. If your partner wants to treat themselves to something small occasionally, consider letting it slide and reserving serious discussions for significant purchases. As long as you're aligned on long-term goals, occasional indulgences won't break the bank.

Lastly, be willing to give your partner the benefit of the doubt. Assuming negative intent will only lead to hurt feelings. Your partner probably has valid reasons for their financial preferences, even if those reasons aren't immediately obvious to you. Make an effort to uncover and understand those reasons without judgment. Through open and compassionate communication, you can navigate and reconcile differing perspectives.

Nurturing Communication and Finding Common Ground

It's important to uncover the underlying concerns and fears that drive your differing financial perspectives, rather than getting caught up in minor arguments. Understanding why each partner handles money the way they do can lead to compromise and mutual respect.

Taking responsibility for financial mistakes, bad habits, or personal quirks is another essential aspect. It's about identifying where you can improve your money management, whether it's a tendency to be overly cautious or a habit of spending without limits.

If you and your partner have disagreements about managing money in areas like budgeting for personal expenses, handling debt, or making investment plans, seeking advice from finance professionals can be valuable. Unbiased expert guidance can help you resolve differences and make informed decisions.

When conflicts arise, finding common financial goals and values can help align your perspectives. Focusing on shared financial objectives and principles can bridge gaps during disagreements by fostering a sense of mutual understanding and purpose.

Additionally, in cases of major differences, discussing potential compromises or blending differing viewpoints can lead to fair solutions that allow you to enjoy the present while safeguarding your financial future. This approach involves coming up with creative solutions that respect and incorporate both partners' preferences.

When significant financial disputes persist despite each person's best efforts, consulting a trustworthy financial counselor or planner can be beneficial. They can provide impartial, personalized advice that leads to a plan that works for both of you. Expert guidance can uncover previously unseen issues and help the couple create a tailored plan that aligns with their unique goals and interests.

It's not constructive to view financial disagreements as harmful to relationships. Instead, consider them as opportunities for better communication, personal growth, and intelligent compromise. Unity and shared objectives are more important than conformity or keeping score. Couples can resolve their financial differences with a collaborative mindset, honesty, and professional advice, fostering genuine unity and mutual respect. When both partners feel their opinions are valued and heard, relationships can thrive, even if their incomes differ. This creates a safe space for understanding and growth.

Engage in Joint Financial Planning

Couples looking to strengthen their financial footing will discover great benefits in working together to manage their money. Instead of handling finances separately, they can transition to a more collaborative and ongoing approach to financial planning. This blending of financial strategies and actions clearly represents the merging of their economic lives into a unified team, emphasizing the significance of shared goals and strategies. However, if one partner is comfortable concentrating on long-term financial goals such as savings and investments while the other prefers managing day-to-day spending, separating financial responsibilities is a viable alternative, as long as it works for both.

Unified Budgeting and Transparent Planning

To make financial planning more seamless, it's important to set up regular monthly or quarterly budget catch-ups. These meetings offer a chance for partners to carefully go over their income and expenses from all sources, discuss upcoming significant expenses, agree on savings goals, and create short- and long-term investment plans. This changes budgeting from a solitary, stress-filled task into a collaborative, team-oriented effort that encourages a joint approach to managing finances.

It's also crucial to maintain shared budgeting tools, documents, and spreadsheets that both partners can easily access. This ensures that all financial information is consolidated and transparent, reducing any secrecy or surprises when it comes to shared finances, which can often lead to distrust and confusion. The importance of mutual transparency cannot be emphasized enough and lays the foundation for a strong financial relationship.

In-Depth Research and Mutual Decisions

When it comes to planning your finances together, it's really important to do some thorough homework before making big personal or household purchases like vacations, cars, homes, renovations, or educational expenses. Looking into things like prices, features, how to pay for them, what you'll get out of them, and other options will help you make smart and well-informed choices. Plus, when you both share your thoughts, it's more likely you'll consider things that one person alone might miss, leading to more well-rounded decisions.

Having in-depth conversations about potential job opportunities is just as crucial, especially when these opportunities could affect your lifestyle due to differences in income, working hours, travel, or other changes. These kinds of discussions are essential for finding the right balance between career growth and a harmonious home life.

Setting and Reviewing Targets

Setting and revisiting financial goals together is essential. These can include things like paying off debts, building an emergency fund, saving for retirement, college expenses, or big purchases. To make these goals effective, get specific—set exact dollar amounts and target dates. It's a good idea to review them at least once a year to adapt to changing needs and priorities.

Goals that become outdated lose their motivating power. Regularly keeping an eye on your goals and adjusting them as necessary keeps both partners actively involved in shaping their financial future.

Short-term goals, like maintaining an emergency fund, should also be checked periodically. After hitting your initial targets, reassess to see if you need more, especially if new risks come up. Avoid the "set and forget" approach with short-term goals.

The key is to make joint goal-setting and reevaluation a regular habit. This way, your targets stay relevant and meaningful, and you and your partner stay motivated. Regularly aligning your goals keeps that motivation high.

Leveraging Professional Guidance

Seeking advice from financial professionals such as advisors, planners, or accountants can be a valuable resource for couples. These experts offer impartial and expert guidance to bring clarity to complex financial matters. Their insights can help couples strike a balance between enjoying the present and securing their future, reducing stress in the process.

Financial professionals can assist in tackling tough decisions, like choosing between saving for retirement or going on a dream vacation. They use their expertise to explore different scenarios and provide recommendations that align with a couple's risk tolerance and time frame, helping them make wise financial choices.

Consistent engagement with a financial planner, rather than one-off consultations, offers continuity. The planner gets to know the couple's complete financial situation, including assets, debts, income, budgets, and responsibilities. This deep understanding allows the planner to provide tailored guidance as circumstances evolve.

Before making significant financial decisions, consulting with an advisor can provide an objective perspective. They may identify risks or considerations that might have been overlooked due to their specialized expertise. Even just confirming that a couple's decision aligns with sound financial principles can offer peace of mind.

Fostering Open Communication

Open and patient communication lies at the heart of united financial planning. It's important for partners to create a supportive atmosphere where they can freely share their perspectives, ideas, concerns, and suggestions without fear of judgment. Listening attentively and considering each other's viewpoints fosters a spirit of collaboration.

In order to be effective financial partners, it's crucial to establish healthy communication habits. Both individuals should feel at ease expressing their financial opinions without worrying about judgment or overreactions. Make financial discussions an open and non-judgmental space.

It's also useful to designate specific times when you can talk about finances without any distractions. Give each other your full attention, actively listen, and aim to understand rather than engage in debates. When disagreements arise, approach them with patience and empathy, and focus on the underlying issues rather than getting caught up in surface arguments.

When making comments, try to educate your partner rather than criticize them. Saying something like "I read that doing X can help improve our credit" is more constructive than saying "You're wrong." Address concerns calmly by using "I feel..." rather than making accusatory "you" statements. You should also avoid blaming each other for past mistakes.

Being receptive to your partner's input creates an environment of financial collaboration. You can brainstorm ideas together, and when necessary, find compromises, always keeping in mind that you share common goals. Fostering mutual respect helps keep your financial discussions positive and productive.

Accommodating Evolving Needs

Couples' financial situations and goals naturally change as life unfolds. It's essential for joint planning to be flexible and able to adjust to these shifts, re-evaluating priorities and realigning goals accordingly.

A couple's financial needs and objectives will evolve with life's twists and turns. Methods that worked early in a relationship might need to be rethought when things like kids, job changes, or other significant life events come into play.

To keep financial planning effective, it must be adaptable and responsive to changing circumstances. As priorities change or new responsibilities emerge, couples should be ready to reevaluate and tweak their financial strategies. Financial plans shouldn't stay fixed in place.

Being willing to periodically update the plan is crucial as needs shift. Staying open-minded and avoiding rigidly sticking to old habits that no longer fit the current situation strengthens financial teamwork over time.

Committing to Ongoing Review

Regularly reviewing your collective budget and goals is important, even when everything seems stable. This practice keeps your financial planning robust and ensures that any emerging needs are identified early and incorporated into your plan before they become urgent problems. It's essential to commit to continuously improving your joint financial strategies.

Make it a habit to have ongoing reviews of your budget and financial goals. You can set calendar reminders to revisit things like insurance policies, investment portfolios, emergency funds, and account beneficiaries.

These periodic check-ins help you spot emerging needs early, preventing them from turning into major issues later on. For instance, increasing life insurance coverage when a new child arrives is a proactive step to avoid being underinsured in the future.

Taking the time to regularly review your finances together, not just during crises, fosters continuous improvement. A partnership in financial stewardship works best when it's an ongoing collaboration, not just a one-time effort. Consistent attention ensures you're ready for whatever life throws your way.

Handle Unsolicited Financial Advice

When couples start their journey into financial planning, they often encounter unsolicited advice from well-meaning sources. This advice can come from different sources, such as well-intentioned parents, friends sharing their own experiences, or colleagues and acquaintances offering tips that have worked for them. These well-meant suggestions can cover a wide range of topics, from job changes to retirement savings strategies.

While these insights are typically rooted in genuine concern and goodwill, they can present challenges, especially when they don't align with the couple's shared financial goals. This misalignment can potentially create unnecessary tension.

Constructing Solid Boundaries and Adopting a Unified Response

The initial and perhaps most crucial step for couples in this situation is to ensure they share a unified perspective. This involves having proactive discussions to outline their approach to potential financial conversations that may arise with family and friends. By anticipating these discussions and crafting a collective response, couples can protect their privacy and spare both partners from unexpected situations where they might feel pressured or cornered.

However, it goes beyond merely having a prepared response. Couples also need to establish clear boundaries, especially when certain individuals frequently offer unsolicited financial advice that diverges from the couple's jointly crafted strategy. While asserting their position, it's important for a couple to strike a balance between standing firm on their decisions while also expressing gratitude for the concern and interest others show. And when repetitive financial discussions threaten to disrupt meaningful interactions, it's often wise to gracefully steer the conversation toward lighter, neutral topics to maintain harmony in the relationship.

Sifting Through Suggestions and Prioritizing Partnership Unity

When receiving unsolicited advice, couples can benefit from taking a thoughtful pause. This pause allows them to carefully consider the offered recommendations in the context of their joint financial goals, deeply held values, risk tolerance, and envisioned milestones.

By looking at these suggestions through a reflective lens, couples can determine which ones to incorporate, which to keep in mind for potential future consideration, and which to politely set aside. In cases where advice strongly contradicts their shared direction, couples can explain their rationale with tact and grace, always prioritizing mutual understanding and unity.

Financial planning isn't just about numbers, it's about trust, understanding, and shared goals. When couples approach this journey collaboratively, it becomes a foundation that strengthens their bond. Such a collaborative spirit, built on mutual trust, open communication, and a shared vision, can significantly fortify their partnership. By intertwining their diverse experiences, consistently making decisions together, and setting and respecting boundaries, couples lay the groundwork for a journey marked by financial stability and relational harmony. Remember, it's not the unsolicited advice that defines the strength of a relationship, but how couples choose to navigate it together.

Understand Your Partner's Financial Traits and Background

It's widely recognized that personal money habits and attitudes are often shaped long before adulthood. Various influences, including family upbringing, cultural backgrounds, significant life events, and socioeconomic status contribute to these ingrained beliefs and behaviors. With this in mind, it's highly beneficial for couples to engage in open conversations about the intricate details of their past financial experiences and influences early in their relationship.

These transparent and vulnerable discussions about finances allow individuals to uncover the layers behind their partner's financial personality, priorities, and sensitivities. Recognizing that these traits are shaped by previous experiences can pave the way for deeper empathy, compromise, and alignment within the relationship.

Delving Into Financial Histories

To get a better grasp of each other's financial backgrounds and quirks, couples can try asking open-ended questions during their conversations. They can dive into the messages they received about money and wealth while growing up, which can reveal whether they saw finances as something scarce or plentiful in their families.

Discussing their biggest money-related fears and worries can provide insight into their vulnerabilities, bringing the couple closer and promoting understanding in the relationship. Taking a moment to think about how their family backgrounds and early money experiences shaped their attitudes and habits can help them figure out which financial approaches they want to adopt or leave behind in their relationship.

Aligning Financial Values and Habits

Moreover, having conversations about core values related to work ethic, how money is managed, generosity, and avoiding debt can help uncover common ground and differences in individual financial values. It's essential to identify the routines or circumstances that bring a sense of financial peace and security, which can serve as a common reference point during financial disagreements.

Assessing the current dynamics of financial management, including whether both partners are actively involved or if one person predominantly handles the day-to-day financial tasks, can clarify the underlying philosophies and preferences in financial management. Additionally, discussing what each partner views as reasonable spending on hobbies, personal allowances, dining out, travel, or other leisure activities can offer insights into their tendencies toward frugality or indulgence.

By dedicating time to these open and exploratory discussions about their past money experiences and influences, couples can achieve a deeper understanding of each other's unique financial personalities and preferences. This enhanced understanding equips them to make informed compromises that respect both backgrounds, allowing them to celebrate shared values and address differences without judgment.

Aligning Major Financial Decisions and Goals

While it's unrealistic for any couple to see eye-to-eye on every single financial decision, maintaining open communication and patience when discussing significant financial choices and goals helps create a shared vision to work toward together. Here are some key steps to outline goals and create a mutual roadmap:

Home Buying

Keep having open chats to figure out what you both want in a home—you can discuss things such as the features you'd love, the neighborhoods that work with your commutes and school needs, how much you can spend based on your income and debts, and if you're leaning toward renting or buying. Decide when you're planning to really start hunting for houses and work out how much to save for a good down payment without dipping into your retirement savings. Also, set a limit on the monthly payment that lets you live comfortably.

It's a good idea to check out model homes together to nail down your "must-haves."

Retirement

Look up data on typical retirement ages and life expectancies to get an idea of when you might realistically retire fully or shift into consulting roles. Use online retirement calculators to figure out how much you should save each month and the investment returns you'd need to ensure you have enough savings to maintain your desired lifestyle.

Read real-life case studies about retirement trends and different lifestyles to get inspired and learn from others' experiences. Chat with your partner about the places you'd like to live and the activities you hope to enjoy as empty nesters and later in life. This will help you paint a picture of your ideal retirement life together.

College

If you're both thinking about saving up for your kids' future college costs, start by considering college savings plans sooner rather than later. This way, you can take advantage of the benefits of tax-deferred growth and compounding.

Decide how much you can comfortably put in each month or year and what exactly you want to cover, like tuition, room and board, or study abroad expenses. This way, you'll be better prepared to tackle those college costs when the time comes.

Insurance

Every now and then, take a look at your life, health, home, disability, umbrella liability, and long-term care insurance policies to see if they still make sense for where you are in life. Make sure your beneficiaries are up to date, and make changes as your family grows and your assets increase.

Debt Payoff

If you're dealing with student loans, car loans, credit card debt, or other financial burdens, make a joint commitment to tackle them head-on. If you can, pay more than just the minimum amount each month to speed up the repayment process and free yourselves from these obligations sooner. Celebrate each time you pay off one of these debts, and aim to live below your means to make meaningful progress.

Major financial goals become more attainable when you brainstorm and plan for them together. Be patient with yourselves when it takes longer than expected to reach these milestones. The journey itself can bring you closer as a couple. Stay motivated and appreciative of any progress you make along the way. Your shared dedication is the key to your success.

Celebrate Meaningful Financial and Career Milestones

As couples navigate life's ups and downs, it's crucial that they take time to appreciate and celebrate financial wins, no matter how big or small. These accomplishments, whether they're the result of hard work, teamwork, or simply good luck, are important markers on your journey together. Pausing to recognize these achievements fosters closeness, gratitude, and an understanding of how your fortunes are intertwined.

For instance, if one of you lands a well-deserved promotion, it's time to celebrate. Maybe go out for a special dinner, plan a weekend getaway, or simply treat yourselves to something you both enjoy. Leaving little notes of congratulations can make this milestone even more special, filling the moment with joy and pride.

Reaching savings goals together, like boosting your retirement accounts through regular contributions, is also something worth celebrating. Celebrating these milestones reinforces your commitment to financial planning and the progress you've made.

Another example of a big accomplishment is paying off stubborn debts, whether it's student loans, car loans, or credit cards. Celebrate by sharing a bottle of champagne and indulging in some delicious desserts. Use this time to talk about the relief and freedom that comes with getting rid of those financial burdens. It's a victory you've achieved together, thanks to your mutual dedication and support.

On special occasions like birthdays, anniversaries, and holidays, taking the time to find or make thoughtful gifts for each other can create lasting memories. Opt for heartfelt, meaningful gifts over extravagant ones to show how much you care. Choose presents that reflect your deep understanding and affection for one another. These gifts, which require time and personal attention, express your true appreciation for each other. Prioritize sentiment over extravagance to highlight your love for your partner, valuing who they are over what you can buy. When it comes to gift-giving, thoughtful generosity speaks louder than materialism.

And if you happen to come into some unexpected money, whether it's from an inheritance, a bonus, a tax refund, or a side business, consider setting some of it aside for shared experiences. Treat yourselves to something special, like a trip abroad, and create beautiful memories that reflect the happiness you both feel about your financial gain.

In your journey toward financial stability, always remember that money is a tool to enhance your connection and pursue shared passions. Reflecting on the progress you've made and the memories you've created together underscores that your relationship is a treasure that's worth more than all the riches in the world. Keep celebrating each other, using milestones as reminders of your shared journey and growth as a couple.

Key Takeaways

See disputes as opportunities to grow in understanding, rather than as threats to the relationship. Listen first, then find healthy compromises.

- **Do Finances Together:** Decide which partner will handle day-to-day spending and which partner will focus on long-term financial goals. Alternatively, you can both choose to manage both aspects. If arguments arise, take a break and revisit the discussion later.

- **Know Money Histories:** Having in-depth discussions about childhood influences, experiences, fears, and lessons learned regarding money provides insight into each other's financial mindsets and personalities.

- **Outline All Goals:** Thoroughly discussing and mapping out shared goals for major upcoming financial targets like home buying, retirement, college savings, and debt repayment creates alignment.

- **Track Milestones:** Taking time to acknowledge and commemorate meaningful markers of financial and career progress together, both big and small, reinforces gratitude, unity, and the intertwined nature of your financial journey.

When couples prioritize transparency, mutual support, and regular financial discussions, they not only secure their financial future but also free up their energy to focus on enhancing their relationship. With this approach, money shifts from being a source of conflict to a tool for realizing shared dreams. Embrace this journey with understanding and excitement for what lies ahead.

Chapter Seven
Keep Love Thriving

Romantic relationships progress through stages, commencing with the blissful honeymoon phase, during which you and your partner can do no wrong in each other's eyes. Nevertheless, as the relationship matures, your partner's flaws start to surface, and vice versa. Yet, this doesn't have to be a negative development. In fact, as the relationship continues to evolve, so does companionship, intimacy, and commitment.

However, if you don't actively invest in each other and your relationship, your daily routines and life's responsibilities can slowly dim the spark, replacing it with stagnation or restlessness.

Couples who thrive together, even after many years, keep that spark alive by creating shared experiences, offering emotional and spiritual support, nurturing meaningful intimacy, reminiscing about cherished memories, and consistently reaffirming their enduring love, affection, and gratitude for each other as life partners.

This chapter delves into practical and effective ways for couples committed to long-lasting love to intentionally strengthen intimacy, open communication, respect, friendship, romance, and personal growth as they journey through life's changing seasons. By establishing meaningful personal and family traditions rooted in their shared story, couples can deepen their emotional connection. These traditions serve as touchpoints for connecting with each other. Furthermore, going on new adventures together renews their sense of partnership and passion, while supporting each other's evolving dreams selflessly allows both individuals to grow with purpose.

Sustaining intimacy through creativity, vulnerability, and attentiveness strengthens the emotional and physical aspects of their relationship. Taking time to fondly reflect on treasured memories ignites gratitude and affection by reliving special moments. Regularly reaffirming their unwavering commitment nourishes a deep soulful connection between partners. Engaging in these intentional practices empowers couples to continuously renew their relationship by reinforcing shared meaning and commitment. Regardless of the obstacles they face, they can rekindle their bond at any stage of their journey.

Every day, choose to passionately recommit to nurturing each other and cherish the precious gift of a love built to last a lifetime together.

Renew Your Vows

If you're a married couple, renewing your vows is a beautiful way to express your love for your spouse. Over the years, as the demands of raising children, pursuing careers, managing bills, and handling numerous responsibilities pile up, it's easy to take your partner for granted or lose sight of the deep connection you shared in the early days of your relationship. One effective remedy for this common relationship challenge is to deliberately keep the flames of love burning bright. You can achieve this by periodically formalizing and reaffirming your choice to be with each other, renewing the sacred vows and dreams you had when you first became a couple.

One wonderful way for couples to rekindle their connection through recommitment is to plan a meaningful ceremony, perhaps on significant anniversaries like their 10th, 20th, or 30th, where they renew their wedding vows in a beautiful setting. Couples can choose to reenact their original wedding or craft new, personalized promises. Many couples find that the act of thoughtfully crafting fresh vows and then publicly declaring their renewed commitment in front of loved ones, after weathering years of ups and downs together, is profoundly moving and emotionally rekindling.

Look for meaningful locations to host your ceremony, like your original wedding venue for a touch of nostalgia, a scenic outdoor spot where you spent your honeymoon, or a spiritual retreat center that holds special meaning in your relationship journey. Write your personalized vows from the heart before the ceremony and surprise each other by reading them aloud while gazing lovingly into each other's eyes. Exchange rings or other meaningful symbols, seal your recommitment with a passionate kiss, and have your loved ones applaud your enduring devotion. Afterward, continue the celebration with a reception dinner, share a slow dance, cut a small vow renewal cake, and listen to heartfelt speeches from friends and family honoring your resilient relationship. Use this momentous occasion to nurture joy and romance that can carry your relationship through the coming decades.

For couples who prefer more intimate ceremonies, consider creating personalized vow renewal certificates or heartfelt letters that explain why you're still deeply devoted to each other after many years. Share what you treasure about your journey together, how your partner's love lifts you daily, and reminisce about special moments that define your love story. Print these letters on quality paper and present them to each other during a private dinner at home, where you can exchange the notes privately and be overwhelmed with emotion at your partner's enduring dedication. Share tearful hugs and passionate kisses and promise to frame these precious words as a reminder that time cannot diminish your love.

In addition to written notes, consider giving your partner meaningful vow renewal gifts on anniversaries such as engraved jewelry, watches, artwork, or figurines symbolizing your lasting commitment. Include personalized messages that reinforce how much this relationship milestone means to you. Or you can surprise your partner by sending a large bouquet of their favorite flowers to their workplace just to see their face light up with surprise and delight. Send them off with a card reiterating that you would choose them all over again each day if given the choice.

Another idea is to write love letters to your partner, recalling your fondest shared memories during especially poignant relationship moments, like the birth of your first child together, buying your dream home after years of saving, witnessing your firstborn graduate from college, or entering exciting new chapters like retirement, when you can finally enjoy more cherished time together after decades of hard work. Use these relationship milestones as opportunities to creatively reaffirm that your love still feels as magical as it did the moment you met your soulmate.

Regardless of the ideas you choose, the key is to make consistent efforts to periodically and creatively reaffirm your mutual commitment, preventing complacency and reigniting the intimacy and devotion reminiscent of new love. While time may challenge even the strongest relationships, yours is worth fighting for. By treasuring and celebrating each other and renewing your promises, your enduring bond will emerge stronger than ever.

Have Occasional "Relationship Holidays"

In addition to renewing vows, couples who thrive together in the long run also intentionally nurture lasting joy and closeness by creating special rituals and celebrations that are unique to their relationship. With creativity, sentiment, and consistency, you can build cherished traditions that symbolize and actively strengthen intimacy, devotion, and friendship over time.

One idea is to choose specific recurring holidays or dates on the calendar as annual opportunities to indulge in and pamper your relationship as a couple. For instance, you could embark on an exciting lovers' adventure getaway every summer solstice. Alternatively, you can create a tradition of displaying old photos and love letters that document your romantic history every Valentine's Day while cooking dinner side by side, followed by slow dancing in the kitchen and massages by candlelight.

On anniversaries, birthdays, and other relationship milestones, find creative ways to transport yourselves nostalgically back to your carefree courtship days together. Recreate aspects of the early dinner dates, lakeside picnic adventures, or moonlit walks that shaped your early love story. Reliving these cherished memories that define the foundation of your relationship can rekindle the starry-eyed wonder and excitement of young love against the backdrop of your mature present.

Other ideas include displaying symbolic keepsakes like framed photos, pressed wildflowers from proposal hikes, ticket stubs from your first concerts and vacations, love letters, seashells from honeymoon beaches, or any other mementos from the places and moments that were pivotal in your journey toward lifelong commitment. Create a relationship memory box or album where these cherished artifacts are collected for reminiscing and reconnecting with the foundation of your shared story. Taking the time to thoughtfully curate this relational history strengthens its legacy.

You can also establish unique ceremonies or rituals together simply because they hold deeper meaning and affirm your enduring bond as partners and soulmates. Traditions might include lighting candles together on anniversaries in honor of your relationship, planting trees or flowers each year to signify your deepening roots as a couple, making lists of why you're grateful for your love, going on sunset strolls to express your thankfulness for another day together, or reading aloud from poetry or literature that conveys your commitment. Even these simple habits, when infused with intention, powerfully reinforce that you're embracing this life adventure hand in hand until the very end.

Establish Ongoing Relationship Rituals

Love goes beyond grand gestures reserved for anniversaries or special occasions. True love radiates through the small, everyday actions that couples take to care for and strengthen their connection. Thoughtful rituals, no matter how seemingly small, lay a sturdy foundation that fortifies the bond over time. Let's delve into how to build this intimate connection.

Cultivate Consistent Connection Time

Life can be a whirlwind, and in the midst of the hustle, it's easy to lose touch. That's why setting aside even a few minutes every day to connect with your partner is crucial. Whether it's savoring your morning coffee together while chatting about your dreams, sharing a calming evening routine, or having a brief phone call during a busy workday, these moments aren't just about talking—they're about truly seeing and being present with each other. This is the heart of staying close amidst life's chaos.

Schedule Weekly Date Nights

While the idea of a "date night" might sound a bit cliché, the core concept remains vital. It's not about sticking to a rigid schedule, it's about regularly rediscovering each other. It could be an evening of dancing, where both of you move to the rhythm, or maybe a mystery dinner theater that keeps you guessing and laughing. But keep in mind, it doesn't always have to mean going out. Preparing a meal from a different culture at home can be a bonding experience, turning your kitchen into a hub of exploration and shared laughter.

The Magic in Daily Habits

Often, it's the little things that create the most meaningful memories. Starting the day with a moment of shared silence, meditation, or prayer can set a harmonious tone. It could be reading to each other before bedtime or jotting down and sharing one positive thing from the day. These small acts are like threads that, when woven together, create the beautiful tapestry of a shared life.

The Joy of Getaways

Stepping away from the daily grind is like hitting a refresh button for relationships. It doesn't have to be a lavish vacation; it could be an impromptu day trip to a nearby charming town, a hike in nature, or even a weekend at a cozy local inn. These getaways serve as a reminder that, beyond your everyday roles, you are fellow adventurers on a shared journey.

Expressions of Affection—The Heart's True Language

Love has a language that doesn't always need words. A surprise hug, an unplanned note slipped into a book, holding hands for no specific reason, or a meaningful, lingering gaze can communicate more than hours of conversation. These heartfelt, everyday gestures act as constant affirmations that the love is flourishing, growing, and profoundly treasured.

Unlocking Hearts through Open Communication

The strength of a relationship often depends on the depth of its conversations. Setting aside moments to talk about dreams, express concerns, share aspirations, and plan for the future are all actions that can strengthen the bond in a relationship. It's about being vulnerably honest, where both partners understand they can open up without fear of judgment.

Growing Together through Shared Skills and Hobbies

Learning and growing together keeps the relationship dynamic and ever-evolving. Whether it's attending a workshop, trying out a new hobby, or even setting a fun challenge for each other every month, these activities foster a spirit of teamwork and shared accomplishment.

In the grand journey of life, it's these rituals and moments that serve as milestones, marking the path of a relationship that's nurtured, cared for, and treasured. Committing to these practices ensures the relationship isn't just enduring but continuously flourishing.

By actively incorporating these rituals into daily life, couples create a robust framework of connection, ensuring the relationship remains vibrant and resilient against the ebb and flow of life's challenges. A consistent dedication to nurturing the bond ensures that love not only survives but thrives.

Engage in Therapeutic Activities Together

In the natural ups and downs of life, daily routines can sometimes become monotonous, potentially straining the bond you share as a couple. To strengthen and rejuvenate this bond, therapeutic activities can serve as a bridge to restore balance and reconnect on a profound level. Here's a closer look at how to integrate these activities into your shared journey:

Prioritize Shared Spa Experiences: Renew and Reconnect

Indulge in a realm of relaxation by scheduling regular spa sessions. Let expert hands dissolve your stresses with synchronized massages in a serene environment. Whether you opt for light conversation or savor shared moments of silence, these spa sessions provide rejuvenating interludes in your busy lives. Beyond the physical relaxation, these experiences offer a sanctuary where you can rekindle your emotional connection, enabling you to reconnect on deeper levels.

Immerse in Therapeutic Indulgences Together

Arrange getaways to peaceful destinations that offer a range of therapeutic indulgences. From the grounding comfort of hot stone massages to immersive sound healing sessions, sharing these unique experiences enhances your connection and provides a joint escape from the daily grind. These retreats are more than mere vacations, they are chances to immerse yourselves in the therapeutic embrace of nature, allowing the surroundings to amplify your bond.

Move and Connect through Restorative Practices

Movement transcends the physical realm; it's a gateway to emotional and spiritual connections. Enroll in classes such as yoga, tai chi, or dance meditations. As you flow, stretch, and breathe in harmony, you'll not only release pent-up anxieties but also rediscover each other in a new light. This shared journey of movement enables both of you to dance the dance of intimacy, where every step, stretch, and breath brings you closer together.

Challenge and Support Each Other's Fitness Goals

Embrace the path to physical improvement as a team. Partner with personal trainers who can lead you through exercises that emphasize flexibility, posture, and alignment. As you support each other through challenges and celebrate every achievement, your joint journey becomes even more memorable.

Rediscover Ancient Healing

Explore the world of traditional Chinese medicine through various healing methods like acupuncture, acupressure, Emotional Freedom Techniques (EFT), Reiki, QiGong, EMDR, and more. These therapies and practices can become a shared path to holistic well-being. As you both find inner harmony, it strengthens your mutual connection.

Cultivate Mindfulness with Shared Meditation

Embark on a journey of meditation together. Whether you decide to sit in stillness, concentrating on each breath, or engage in profound, soulful eye contact, these instances of shared silence communicate deeply. Clear your minds and harmonize with each other's inner energies. As you incorporate these therapeutic activities into your relationship, they not only contribute to your personal well-being but also become woven into the rich tapestry of shared experiences that nourish and strengthen your connection.

Participate in Couples' Counseling and Enrichment

Proactively seeking professional help before relationship struggles escalate provides couples with valuable insights and communication strategies to navigate challenges in a healthy way.

Consider engaging in counseling or attending intensive enrichment retreats. You can also regularly meet with a licensed marriage counselor or therapist, even during stable periods, to address underlying conflicts related to intimacy, trust, or family dynamics that could erode the relationship's foundation. Healing past relational wounds can restore a vibrant connection.

Counseling offers constructive support and feedback, helping you deepen your relationship rather than succumbing to complacency. Another option is to explore intensive couples' workshops available at counseling centers and faith-based organizations. These programs provide comprehensive education on essential relationship skills. Instead of avoiding conflict, they teach constructive methods for addressing it. By delving into each other's love languages, you can enhance your intimacy. It's essential to cultivate practices like forgiveness and gratitude, which strengthen your connection. It's important to face challenges—whether it's balancing the desire for closeness with the need for independence or navigating stressors like infertility—with patience and mutual support. Dealing with past relational traumas through understanding and clear communication makes healing achievable. If you're blending families after remarriage, approach it with compassion. Even as the initial passion wanes after the honeymoon phase, these workshops empower you to reignite that spark. Participating in these sessions with an open heart and mind enables couples to internalize insights and foster a collaborative spirit. Commit to applying these teachings in your daily life, and your relationship will thrive through shared growth.

Participate together in couples' enrichment retreats held in serene natural settings. During these multi-day getaways, licensed counselors guide couples through sessions on topics like wholeheartedness in relationships, secure emotional attachment, resolving conflicts productively, rebuilding intimacy and trust after affairs, expressing your authentic self in a safe space, becoming your spouse's trusted confidante, and more. The combination of expert guidance and dedicated time away from distractions allows couples to achieve breakthroughs. Couples often return from these retreats renewed.

It's vital to invest in your lifelong relationship by dedicating time to regular checkups, maintenance, and care, much like you would for your physical health. Seeking professional counseling periodically helps uncover and address unhealthy patterns before they endanger the relationship. Value your love enough to nurture its continuous growth.

Discover New Activities and Pursuits Together

To reignite the passion in your relationship, couples can intentionally step out of their comfort zones and engage in new, unfamiliar pursuits together. Sharing novel experiences recaptures the excitement of your early days together. Here are some ideas to rekindle your passion for each other:

Embrace New Adventures

Sparking excitement in a relationship can be achieved by trying thrilling physical activities that neither of you has experienced before. Dive into the deep blue sea with scuba diving, ride the waves while surfing, or feel an adrenaline rush by ziplining over cascading waterfalls. These activities not only reintroduce adventure into your lives but also provide opportunities to support and rely on each other in fresh and exhilarating ways.

Cultivate Shared Skills

Learning a new skill together can be a wonderful way to bond through shared experiences and mutual progress. You can explore the art of winemaking, take a ballroom dancing class, or unleash your creativity in pottery and woodworking. As you both transition from being beginners to becoming skilled in your chosen pursuit, the joy comes not only from mastering the skill but also from witnessing each other's growth and development.

Find Purpose in Serving Others

Engaging in acts of kindness and service together is another wonderful way to fortify your connection. Consider volunteering for organizations that align with your shared values, whether it's providing meals to the homeless, assisting in the care of rescued animals, or participating in community housing projects. The deep satisfaction that comes from making a positive impact side by side is a profound and rewarding experience.

Discover Global Cultures at Home

Broaden your horizons and strengthen your connection by diving into the colorful tapestry of global cultures. Take a fun learning journey like diving into language classes together. Whether you're enchanted by the melodic sounds of Italian or captivated by the fascinating characters of Arabic, shared learning of unfamiliar cultures can help nurture the bond in a relationship. Another idea is to spice things up with culinary experiments, from trying out Indian flavors to becoming sushi-making pros. These joint cultural adventures will not only expand your worldviews but also deepen your bond as you navigate and savor the diverse tastes of the world side by side.

Indulge in Creative Exploration

There's a certain magic in creating and appreciating beauty together. Enroll in photography courses to capture fleeting moments, let watercolor paints tell your tales, or immerse yourselves in melodious singing workshops. Additionally, visiting galleries, attending concerts, or simply soaking in various art forms can be deeply inspiring and rejuvenating.

Navigate New Horizons Hand-in-Hand

These activities are all about delving into the uncharted together, pushing your limits, and always finding fresh facets of each other. As you both dive headfirst into these escapades, the world will begin to glow with more vibrancy and color. Each shared escapade, every hurdle you conquer, and all the new skills you pick up together add even more sparkle to your connection. Keep treasuring this adventure, and keep falling in love with life and each other every step of the way.

Support and Share in Individual Dreams and Aspirations

Couples who thrive together, even after many years, find joy and pride in nurturing each other's personal growth and evolving passions. Wholeheartedly support your partner as they chase their long-held dreams, and always be your partner's biggest cheerleader.

When your partner discovers new interests and talents, be their encouragement, and don't let complacency or jealousy get in the way. Help them take small steps toward honing their skills and sharing their gifts.

If your partner decides to make a bold career change to pursue more meaningful work, stand by them through the uncertainties and financial challenges of the transition. Embrace their yearning for purpose and provide unwavering emotional support.

When your partner is passionate about launching a new business idea, brainstorm together to refine strategies and work through challenges, focusing on the possibilities rather than the risks. Help them build the wings they need to soar toward their entrepreneurial dreams.

If your partner finds their calling in volunteer work, make an effort to accommodate their schedule and ask how you can contribute to their cause. Use your unique skills to reinforce their efforts.

Whether they're learning to play the piano, buying a boat to explore waterways, starting a nonprofit to help the local community, writing poetry, or getting into backyard beekeeping, it is important to show interest and find both big and small ways to uplift your partner. Instead of holding them back, give them the freedom to become their best self. Sometimes, all dreams need is someone who steadfastly believes in them. Be that person. Support is a tangible expression of love.

Respect and Encourage Personal Growth

As partners grow and change over the years, supporting each other's journey allows you both to become your best selves. Here are some ways to embrace each other's unfolding:

Welcome Your Partner's Unfolding

When your partner discovers new passions or parts of themselves, welcome these rather than restrict them. Offer empathy as they process changes. If they challenge you to grow where you've been defensive, reflect openly. Their insight could heal your wounds. It is important to encourage their progress with grace, celebrate when they find new aspects of themselves, make space for their revelations without limiting them, and give heartfelt understanding as they integrate changes.

Support Your Partner through Transitions

When life forces your partner to redirect energy, be their rock in difficult times. Help them redefine purpose with courage. Adjust your pace to walk with them through challenges and offer steadfast support through every transition, no matter how turbulent.

Respect Your Partner's Choice of Path

If their growth departs from your vision, release control. Support their right to chart their course. Trust that different roads can reach the same destination, and make space for them to evolve. It's crucial that you allow change without resentment, expand your capacity for uncertainty, and keep your heart open to life's surprises.

Embrace the Journey Together

Encourage your partner's growth with grace and celebrate the progress and passions they discover along the way. Embrace their journey of self-discovery, making room for their revelations and personal evolutions. Where barriers once stood in their path, it's important that you help your partner let them crumble and assist in mending their wounds with understanding and kindness. Be your partner's steadfast support during times of change, and bravely help them redefine his purpose. As you both navigate challenges, remember to relinquish the need to control their every step.

Recognize that your partner might take different paths but with the same end goal in mind, fostering an environment where they feel free to question, evolve, and truly find themselves. Embrace the unknown on behalf of your partner, expand your tolerance for life's uncertainties, and always remain open to its surprises. Through every twist and turn, stay by their side, supporting them wherever his journey might lead.

Revisit Meaningful Places from Your Shared History

Revisiting old memories together can bring back positive memories and make new ones. Mindfully reconnecting with places that hold meaning for both of you adds a fresh perspective to your journey as a couple.

Remember Your Beginnings

While on vacation, make it a point to visit places that played a role in the early days of your courtship, wedding festivities, honeymoon adventures, or other treasured moments you've shared. Allow nostalgia to sweep over you as you journey back to the origins of your love story. Take in the distance you've traveled since those initial, tender steps. Relive your dearest memories by returning to the locations where your romance first blossomed. Deliberately plan getaways to destinations that mark significant milestones, such as your wedding, honeymoon, or the start of your love story. Allow yourself to be completely immersed in nostalgia, and reflect on how much you've grown since those early chapters.

Return to Your Roots

Take a trip back to your old neighborhood haunts. Look at the house or apartment where you first started building your love nest. Remember the dreams, the doubts, and the sweet beginnings you shared under that roof. Feel the growth that's happened since you first put down roots there. Drive to your very first shared home. Take a peek at the apartment that witnessed the start of your love story.

Reflect on the foundations you laid, the dreams you nurtured, and the uncertainties you faced together under one roof. Appreciate how deeply your roots have grown intertwined.

Revisit Special Spots

Take your partner to meaningful places like the lake where you first held hands, the church where you exchanged vows, the hospital where your children were born, or the garden where you shared your first kiss. Let the stories embedded in the earth and stone come alive. Revisit your favorite restaurants, parks, beaches, or past getaways. Relive the laughter, conversations, and amazement you once shared in those spots. Walk together once more around the lake where you first held hands. Pass by the hospital where you first held your child. Take a leisurely stroll through the garden that witnessed your first kiss. Reconnect with the places that hold your cherished memories. Share the stories that are etched there.

Gain Strength from the Past

No matter how much time has passed, mindfully reconnecting with places of shared importance offers a fresh perspective on how your relationship has evolved over the years. Express gratitude to each other for the journey you've taken since the times you shared in those special places. Let the love that started it all years ago be a source of strength for today. As the years go by, revisiting meaningful locations together continues to breathe new life into your connection. These trips down memory lane provide a fresh view of your changing relationship landscape. Be thankful for the growth you've experienced since you first ventured there, and draw strength from the love that initially brought you together to nurture your bond today. Cherish how you've grown together over time.

Celebrate Anniversaries and Special Occasions

Building special traditions to celebrate anniversaries, birthdays, and other unique occasions keeps couples connected and joyful throughout the years. It's important that you mark your milestones with genuine love and appreciation.

Cherish Your Anniversary

Anniversaries can be celebrated in various ways, and the preferences of CD and MY men can differ.

CD men may prefer low-key celebrations, like enjoying a home-cooked meal together. To make it even more special, you could recreate the meal you had on your wedding day. After dinner, you can reminisce by looking through your wedding album, watching your wedding video, or sharing a slow dance to your first song.

On the other hand, MY men may opt for a more extravagant celebration. They might enjoy gathering with friends and family at a restaurant, brewery, or winery. Alternatively, they may relish taking a day trip or spending a weekend away.

Both CD and MY men might also appreciate returning to their honeymoon destination, reading their original vows aloud, exchanging gifts and heartfelt notes, or lighting candles from their wedding ceremony.

Make Birthdays Special

Make birthdays special by giving experiences that match your partner's current interests, like tickets to see their favorite band, a hot air balloon ride, a couple's spa retreat, or gourmet cooking classes. Wrap your gifts with inside jokes based on old traditions; it's a way to show how well you understand them.

Recreate Your First Date Night

Valentine's Day is that special time of year to relive your very first official date, complete with the same food, activities, and ambiance. Swap handwritten love notes, and remember that celebrating your love is the top priority.

Make Each Milestone Meaningful

Whatever the occasion, fill it with heartfelt touches that show just how much your partner matters to you. Your sincere devotion carries more weight than any material gift. Celebrate the precious gift of traveling through life together. As you reach each milestone, craft special traditions that strengthen your connection as the years go by.

Key Takeaways

The advice offered in this chapter can be put into practice to foster a lifetime of intimacy and growth between partners throughout the lifetime of their relationship. To maintain the vitality of love in all you do, remember to:

- **Cherish Rituals:** Establish meaningful relationship traditions, holidays, and rituals that reinforce your bond.

- **Renew Devotion and Vows:** Proactively renew vows and exchange other symbols of commitment.

- **Seek Enrichment:** Seek counseling and participate in intensive couples' enrichment experiences together.

- **Pursue Bold Adventures:** Discover new passions, activities, and pursuits alongside your partner to keep life vibrant.

- **Support Dreams:** Encourage and support each other's evolving personal dreams, callings, and growth.

- **Nurture Your Souls:** Engage in therapeutic activities like couples' massages and meditation that reconnect you.

- **Revisit Memories:** Return together to places of shared significance from your relationship history.

- **Celebrate Anniversaries:** Personalize anniversary and milestone traditions to commemorate your journey.

No matter your stage of life, purposefully nurture your connection through shared experiences. It's important to recommit to each other daily as your love story continues.

Chapter Eight

Final Thoughts

In the boundless landscape of human connections, love rises as one of our most profound yet complex experiences. It's far more than fleeting passion or giddy infatuation; love is a commitment to growth and understanding.

In these pages, we have embarked on an enlightening expedition through the intricate world of loving a Cave Dweller or Mountain Yeller man. Now, let us pause to appreciate all we have learned on this odyssey of the heart.

Understanding the Depth of Personality

Every person is a unique cosmos of thoughts, emotions, and perspectives, but that doesn't mean that common traits can't be identified.

Your CD man may find sanctuary in silent spaces, his introspective nature thriving inwardly, while your MY partner revels in lively social spheres, expressing himself outwardly with zeal. Though seemingly opposite, these differences serve the same end goal: expressing oneself and one's love. Remember the importance of active listening, appreciating quietude, and offering verbal affirmations. These are not merely communication tips. They are passageways to comprehension, empathy, and soulful connection. Peeling back the layers to see someone's authentic essence is the pinnacle of intimacy.

The Unwavering Commitment of Love

Love is not demonstrated by way of grand gestures alone. It requires a daily renewal of choice. Recall the tools we discovered together—from reconfirming vows, planning surprise dates, and engaging in couples therapy, to prioritizing quality time. These are not just actions but representations of an unwavering commitment to nurture the living, breathing bond you share. Like a flowering plant, love requires daily care and watering to continue blossoming.

The Adaptive Nature of Lasting Love

Change is inevitable, and in relationships, it can signify growth, wisdom, and mutual understanding. Consider the dance between CD and MY personalities—their harmony requires flexibility, balance, and adjustment. Our discussions around financial planning and establishing traditions and rituals were about more than checking tasks off a list. These actions will help you to embrace change, adapt together, and find joy in that evolution.

Celebrate Diversity through Unity

Do opposites attract? They certainly can! There is remarkable splendor in two distinct souls coming together to write a shared story. The fusion of a CD's introspection with an MY's exuberance breeds something uniquely beautiful. Remember our conversations on custom anniversary celebrations, trying new hobbies, and revisiting meaningful places? These are not just moments, but milestones where differences unite to create harmonious new memories.

The Journey of Mutual Growth

Growth is the essence of life. In relationships, it is the adhesive binding two people through time. Reflect on the times you have buoyed your partner's ambitions, championed their dreams, or embarked on a quest of self-discovery side-by-side. It is about acknowledging that as individuals, and as a couple, there is always room for progress, adaptation, and cultivation into better versions of oneself.

The Evolution of Your Love Story

As we conclude, remember that your love is an unfolding narrative, filled with twists, turns, peaks, and valleys. Your shared experiences, growth, and obstacles render it beautifully yours. Internalize the wisdom gained, cherish each moment, and eagerly anticipate the countless memories yet to be created. Love, in all its intricacies, is a sojourn worth embracing wholeheartedly.

This book isn't titled *"The* 50 Ways to Love Your Man" for one simple reason: the number of ways to show your love is limitless. Find new ones to today...

Appendices

Self-Assessment Questionnaire: Determine if You're a CD, MY, or Straddler

In the quest for self-understanding, recognizing one's intrinsic personality traits plays a crucial role. This self-assessment questionnaire has been carefully designed to help you discern whether you align most closely with the introspective nature of a Cave Dweller (CD), the extroverted inclinations of a Mountain Yeller (MY), or the balanced characteristics of a Straddler. By reflecting on your behaviors, preferences, and reactions in various situations, this tool aims to provide insight into your predominant personality type. Approach each question with honesty and openness, and remember, there's no right or wrong answer—just a deeper understanding of your unique self waiting to be unveiled.

Personality Indicator #1

Circle one answer per question.

1. Have you ever walked in your sleep during your adult life?

   YES or NO

2. As a teenager, did you feel comfortable expressing your feelings to one or both of your parents?

   YES or NO

3. Do you have a tendency to look directly into a person's eyes when talking to them?

   YES or NO

4. Do you feel that most people, when you first meet them, are uncritical of your appearance?

   YES or NO

5. In a group situation with people you've just met, would you feel comfortable drawing attention to yourself by initiating a conversation?

   YES or NO

6. Do you feel comfortable holding hands or hugging someone you're in a relationship with in front of other people?

   YES or NO

7. When someone talks about feeling warm physically, do you begin to feel warm also?

   YES or NO

8. Do you tend to tune out when someone is talking to you because you're anxious to come up with your side of the story?

   YES or NO

9. Do you feel that you learn better by seeing and/or reading than by hearing?

   YES or NO

10. In a new class or company meeting, do you usually feel comfortable asking questions in front of the group?

    YES or NO

11. When expressing your ideas, do you find it important to relate all the details leading up to the subject so the other person can understand it completely?

    YES or NO

12. Do you enjoy relating to children?

    YES or NO

13. Are you comfortable with your body movements when faced with unfamiliar people and circumstances?

YES or NO

14. Do you prefer reading fiction rather than non-fiction?

    YES or NO

15. If you were to imagine sucking on a juicy lemon, would your mouth water?

    YES or NO

16. Do you feel comfortable receiving a compliment in front of other people?

    YES or NO

17. Do you feel that you're a good conversationalist?

    YES or NO

18. Do you feel comfortable when complimentary attention is drawn to your physical body?

    YES or NO

Personality Indicator # 2

Circle one answer per question.

1. Have you ever awakened in the middle of the night and felt that you could not move your body and/or talk?

   YES or NO

2. As a child, did you feel you were more affected by your parents' tone of voice than by what they actually said?

YES or NO

3. If someone you know talks about a fear that you've experienced before, do you have a tendency to re-experience that apprehension or fear?

YES or NO

4. After having an argument with someone, do you tend to dwell on what you could or should have said?

YES or NO

5. Do you tend to occasionally tune out when someone is talking to you and therefore don't hear what's being said because your mind drifts to something totally unrelated?

YES or NO

6. Do you sometimes desire to be complimented for a job well done, but feel embarrassed or uncomfortable when complemented?

YES or NO

7. Do you often fear not being able to carry on a conversation with someone you've just met?

YES or NO

8. Do you feel self-conscious when attention is drawn to your

physical body or appearance?

YES or NO

9. If you had a choice, would you rather avoid being around children most of the time?

YES or NO

10. Do you feel uptight in body movements, especially when faced with unfamiliar people or circumstances?

YES or NO

11. Do you prefer reading non-fiction rather than fiction?

YES or NO

12. If someone describes a very bitter taste, do you have difficulty experiencing the physical feeling of that bitter taste?

YES or NO

13. Do you generally feel that you see yourself less favorably than others see you?

YES or NO

14. Do you tend to feel awkward or self-conscious holding hands and/or kissing someone you're in a relationship with, in front of other people?

YES or NO

15. In a new lecture or company meeting, do you usually feel uncomfortable asking questions in front of the group?

    YES or NO

16. Do you feel uneasy if someone you've just met looks you directly in the eyes when talking to you, especially if the conversation is about you?

    YES or NO

17. In a group situation with people you've just met, would you feel uncomfortable drawing attention to yourself by initiating a conversation?

    YES or NO

18. If you're in a relationship or are very close to someone, do you find it difficult or embarrassing to verbalize your love for them?

    YES or NO

Personality Indicator Scores

Personality Indicator #1

- Give yourself 10 points for every yes answer for questions one and two.
- Give yourself 5 points for every YES answer for questions three through eighteen.

- Write the total number at the top of #1's questionnaire.

Personality Indicator #2

- Give yourself 10 points for every yes answer for questions one and two.

- Give yourself 5 points for every YES answer for questions three through eighteen.

- Write the total number at the top of #2's questionnaire.

- Combine the total from PI 1 & 2.

Using the Scoring Chart

- On the scoring chart, look up the combined score of Personality Indicators 1 & 2 on the HORIZONTAL axis of the chart and circle the number.

- Take the total score of PI #1, locate it on the VERTICAL axis of the chart, and circle the number.

- Draw a horizontal line across the page from the PI 1 score, then draw a vertical line down from the combined score.

- The number in the box where the two lines intersect represents your true, adjusted percentage personality indicator.

- Scores 61 and higher indicate a Mountain Yeller personality type.

- Scores 45 and lower indicate a Cave Dweller personality type.

- Scores 47 to 56 indicate a Straddler personality type.

Cave Dweller Tendencies

- Reserved
- Head ruled
- Controlling
- Wants space and security
- Prefers socializing one-on-one
- Singular focus
- Thinks before reacting
- Prefers showing affection privately
- Distrusts flattery
- Enjoys working alone
- Enjoys individual activities
- Wants alone time
- Dresses for comfort
- Decides after thinking about it
- Speaks literally, to the point
- Infers from what others say
- Feels emotional pain in the mind

- Fears loss of security

Cave Dweller Priorities

- Career/Financial Security
- Hobbies/Children
- Relationships/Family
- Sex/Lovers

Mountain Yeller Tendencies

- Outgoing
- Heart ruled
- Dominating
- Wants connection and touch
- Enjoys socializing in groups
- Movement focused
- Reacts spontaneously
- Comfortable with affection anytime
- Likes reassurance and compliments
- Enjoys working with people
- Enjoys team activities

- Wants to be together as much as possible
- Decides in the moment
- Speaks inferentially—adds story
- Takes literally what others say
- Feels emotional pain in body and mind
- Fears rejection

Mountain Yeller Priorities

- Relationships/Sex
- Family/Children
- Friends/Hobbies
- Career/Financial security

COMBINED SCORE #1 AND #2

SCORE #1 \ #2	50	55	60	65	70	75	80	85	90	95	100	105	110	115	120	125	130	135	140	145	150	155	160	165	170	175	180	185	190	195	200
100											100	95	91	87	83	80	77	74	71	69	67	65	63	61	59	57	56	54	53	51	50
95											100	95	90	86	83	79	76	73	70	68	66	63	61	59	58	56	54	53	51	50	49	48
90											100	95	90	86	82	78	75	72	69	67	64	62	60	58	56	55	53	51	50	49	47	46	45
85									100	94	89	85	81	77	74	71	68	65	63	61	59	57	55	53	52	50	49	47	46	45	44	43
80								100	94	89	84	80	76	73	70	67	64	62	59	57	55	53	52	50	48	47	46	44	43	42	41	40
75							100	94	88	83	79	76	71	68	65	63	60	58	56	54	52	50	48	47	45	44	43	42	41	39	38	38
70						100	93	88	82	78	74	70	67	64	61	58	56	54	52	50	48	47	45	44	42	41	40	39	38	37	36	35
65					100	93	87	81	76	72	68	65	62	59	57	54	52	50	48	46	45	43	42	41	39	38	37	36	35	34	33	33
60				100	92	86	80	75	71	67	63	60	57	55	52	50	48	46	44	43	41	40	39	38	36	35	34	33	32	32	31	30
55			100	92	85	79	73	69	65	61	58	55	52	50	48	46	44	42	41	39	38	37	36	34	33	32	31	31	30	29	28	28
50		100	91	83	77	71	67	63	59	56	53	50	48	45	43	42	40	38	37	36	34	33	32	31	30	29	28	27	26	26	26	25
45	90	82	75	69	64	60	56	53	50	47	45	43	41	39	38	36	35	33	32	31	30	29	28	27	26	26	25	24	24	23	23
40	80	73	67	62	57	53	50	47	44	42	40	38	36	35	33	32	31	30	29	28	27	26	25	24	24	23	22	22	21	21	20
35	70	64	58	54	50	47	44	41	39	37	35	33	32	31	30	29	28	27	26	25	24	23	23	22	21	21	20	19	19	18	18	18
30	60	55	50	46	43	40	38	36	33	32	30	29	27	26	25	24	23	22	21	21	20	19	19	18	18	17	17	16	16	15	15
25	50	45	42	38	36	33	31	29	28	26	25	24	23	22	21	20	19	19	18	17	17	16	15	15	14	14	14	13	13	13
20	40	38	33	31	29	27	25	24	22	21	20	19	18	17	16	15	15	14	13	13	13	12	12	11	11	11	11	10	10
15	30	27	25	23	21	20	19	18	17	16	15	14	14	13	12	12	11	11	10	10	9	9	9	8	8	8	8	8
10	20	18	17	15	14	13	13	12	11	11	10	10	9	9	8	8	7	7	7	7	6	6	6	6	6	5	5	5	5
5	10	9	8	8	7	7	6	6	6	5	5	5	5	4	4	4	4	4	3	3	3	3	3	3	3	3	3	3	3
0	0	0	0	0	0	0	0	0	0	0	0	0	0	0	0	0	0	0	0	0	0	0	0	0	0	0	0	0	0	0	0

About the Author

Dr. Cline lives with her husband, two daughters, two German Shepherds, and two Yorkies in the hills of North Carolina. Her expertise in relationship building has offered her the opportunity to travel around the world as a keynote speaker and international workshop facilitator.

www.ingramcontent.com/pod-product-compliance
Lightning Source LLC
Chambersburg PA
CBHW070106080526
44586CB00013B/1207